Making It New

Making It New

EDITED BY
JoAn E. Chace
William M. Chace—Stanford University

CANFIELD PRESS ⌽
SAN FRANCISCO, CALIFORNIA
A DEPARTMENT OF HARPER & ROW, PUBLISHERS, INC.
NEW YORK · EVANSTON · LONDON

MAKING IT NEW
Copyright © 1973 by JoAn E. Chace and William M. Chace

Printed in the United States of America. All Rights Reserved.

No part of this book may be used or reproduced in any manner whatsoever without permission except in the case of brief quotations embodied in critical articles and reviews. For information address Harper & Row Publishers, Inc., 49 East 33rd Street, New York, N.Y. 10016.

Standard Book Number: 0-06-382485-X

Library of Congress Catalog Card Number: 72-805-84

73 74 75 10 9 8 7 6 5 4 3 2

Part opening and cover drawings by Robert Bausch
Cover and interior design by Ted Ricks

Acknowledgments

We want to thank the following people for helping us with information or advice: Donald Davie and Sotère Torregian of Stanford University; William J. Harris and Frank Cady, graduate students at Stanford; David Weiss, student at the University of California, Berkeley; George Xanttopoulos, student at Stanford University; Robert J. Griffin of the California State College, Hayward; Rusty Driscoll, painter, San Francisco; Peter Collier of *Ramparts* magazine; and Ted Ricks of Canfield Press.

The following books or periodicals were especially useful: *Contemporary Poets of the English Language*, ed. Rosalie Murphy (Chicago: St. James Press, 1970); Lillian Roxon, *Rock Encyclopedia* (New York: Workman/Grosset and Dunlap, 1969); *Rolling Stone*; Nat Shapiro, *Popular Music an Annotated Index of American Popular Songs* (New York: Adrian Press, 1964; later volumes 1965, 1967, 1968, 1969); and John Chilton, *Who's Who of Jazz Storyville to Swing Street* (London: The Bloomsbury Book Shop, 1970).

The skill of reference librarians of the Stanford University libraries was invaluable to us. We should like to thank, especially, William Allen, James Knox, and Elizabeth Rebman.

We gratefully acknowledge the following authors and publishers:

John Balaban, "The Guard at the Binh Thuy Bridge," from *Vietnam Poems* by John Balaban. Copyright © 1968 by the New York Times Company. Reprinted by permission of John Balaban.

Imamu Amiri Baraka (LeRoi Jones), "I Substitute for the Dead Lecturer," from *The Dead Lecturer* by LeRoi Jones. Copyright © 1964 by LeRoi Jones, reprinted by permission of The Sterling Lord Agency, Inc. "A Poem Some People Will Have to Understand"; "Red Light"; "Poem for Halfwhite College Students"; "Loku"; and, "American Ecstasy" from *Black Magic Poetry 1961-1967,* copyright © 1969, by LeRoi Jones, reprinted by permission of the publisher, The Bobbs-Merrill Company, Inc.

Robert Bly, "Driving Toward the Lac Qui Parle River," and "Ode to My Socks (Pablo Neruda)," reprinted from *Silence in the Snowy Fields,* Wesleyan University Press, 1962, copyright © 1962 by Robert Bly, reprinted by permission of the author. "Looking into a Face"; "Come with Me"; "Hatred of Men with Black Hair"; "Counting Small-Boned Bodies"; and, "Sleet Storm on the Merritt Parkway," from *Light Around the Body* by Robert Bly. Copyright © 1962 by Robert Bly. Reprinted by permission of Harper & Row, Publishers, Inc. Section II pages 9-12, section IV pages 19-20, from *The Teeth Mother Naked at Last* by Robert Bly. Copyright © 1970 by Robert Bly. Reprinted by permission of City Lights Books.

Gwendolyn Brooks, "Sadie and Maud," from *The World of Gwendolyn Brooks* by Gwendolyn Brooks. Copyright © 1945 by Gwendolyn Brooks Blakely. "Jessie Mitchell's Mother," from *The World of Gwendolyn Brooks* by Gwendolyn Brooks. Copyright © 1960 by Gwendolyn Brooks. "We Real Cool," from *The World of Gwendolyn Brooks* by Gwendolyn Brooks. Copyright © 1959 by Gwendolyn Brooks. "Beverly Hills, Chicago," from *The Womanhood* (section VIII) by Gwendolyn Brooks. Copyright © 1949 by Gwendolyn Brooks Blakely. Reprinted by permission of Harper & Row, Publishers, Inc.

Lucille Clifton, "In the Inner City"; "Good Times"; "Ca'line's Prayer"; "For deLawd"; and, "Admonitions," from *Good Times,* by Lucille Clifton. Copyright © 1969 by Lucille Clifton. Reprinted by permission of Random House, Inc.

Sam Cooke, "A Change Is Gonna Come," by Sam Cooke. Copyright © 1964 and 1967 by Kags Music Corp. Reprinted by permission of Kags Music Corp. All rights reserved. International copyright secured. "A Change Is Gonna Come," by Otis Redding. Copyright © 1964 and 1967 by Kags Music Corp. Reprinted by permission of Kags Music Corp. All rights reserved. International Copyright secured.

Gregory Corso, "Last Night I Drove a Car" and, "Sun," from *Gasoline* by Gregory Corso. Copyright © 1958 by Gregory Corso. Reprinted by permission of City Lights Books. "Friend," from *Long Live Man* by Gregory Corso. Copyright © 1959, 1962 by New Directions Publishing Corporation. "Marriage," from *The Happy Birthday of Death* by Gregory Corso. Copyright © 1960 by New Directions Publishing Corporation. Reprinted by permission of New Directions Publishing Corporation.

Robert Creeley, "If You"; "Oh No"; and, "I Know a Man," from *For Love* by Robert Creeley. Copyright © 1962 by Robert Creeley. "The Rhythm"; and "Anger," from *Words* by Robert Creeley. Copyright © 1962 by Robert Creeley. Reprinted by permission of Charles Scribner's Sons.

Victor Hernández Cruz, "& Stuff Like That"; "Is a Dead Man"; and, "Latin & Soul," from *Snaps* by Victor Hernández Cruz. Copyright © 1968, 1969 by Victor Hernández Cruz. Reprinted by permission of Random House, Inc.

E. E. Cummings, "Since Feeling Is First," from *Is 5* by E. E. Cummings. Copyright © renewed 1953 by E. E. Cummings. Reprinted by permission of Liveright, New York. "I Sing of Olaf Glad and Big," from *Poems 1923-1954* by E. E. Cummings. Copyright © E. E. Cummings. Reprinted by permission of Harcourt Brace Jovanovich, Inc.

James Dickey, "Cherrylog Road," from *Poems 1957-1967* by James Dickey. Copyright © 1963 by James Dickey. First published in *The New Yorker*. Reprinted by permission of Wesleyan University Press.

Robert Duncan, "Nel Mezzo del Cammin di Nostra Vita," from *Roots and Branches* by Robert Duncan. Copyright © 1964 by Robert Duncan. "The Multiversity, Passages 21," from *Bending the Bow* by Robert Duncan. Copyright © 1968 by Robert Duncan. Reprinted by permission of New Directions Publishing Corporation.

Bob Dylan, "Blowin' in the Wind," by Bob Dylan. Copyright © 1962 by M. Witmark & Sons. "Subterranean Homesick Blues," by Bob Dylan. Copyright © 1965 by M. Witmark & Sons. "It Ain't Me, Babe," and "Mr. Tambourine Man," by Bob Dylan. Copyright © 1964 by M. Witmark & Sons. Used by Permission of Warner Bros. Music. All Rights Reserved. "If Dogs Run Free," by Bob Dylan. Copyright © 1969 by Big Sky Music. "Lay, Lady, Lay," by Bob Dylan. Copyright © 1970 by Big Sky Music. Used by permission of Big Sky Music.

Florence Elon, "Visiting Hours," by Florence Elon. Copyright © by the *Canadian Forum*. Reprinted by permission of *Canadian Forum*. Previously printed in *Canadian Forum*. "Berlin: the Ruined Countess," from *The Massachusetts Review*. Copyright © 1966 by The Massachusetts Review, Inc. Reprinted by permission of The Massachusetts Review, Inc.

Lawrence Ferlinghetti, "In Goya's Greatest Scenes We Seem to See," from *A Coney Island of the Mind* by Lawrence Ferlinghetti. Copyright © 1958 by Lawrence Ferlinghetti. "After the Cries of the Birds," from *The Secret Meaning of Things* by Lawrence Ferlinghetti. Copyright © 1966 by Lawrence Ferlinghetti. Reprinted by permission of New Directions Publishing Corporation.

Edward Field, "Graffiti" and, "Unwanted," from *Stand Up, Friend, With Me* by Edward Field. Copyright © 1963 by Edward Field. "Frankenstein"; "The Bride of Frankenstein"; and, "The Return of Frankenstein," from *Variety Photoplays* by Edward Field. Copyright © 1967 by Edward Field. Reprinted by permission of Grove Press, Inc.

Allen Ginsberg, "A Supermarket in California"; "Sunflower Sutra," and, "America," from *Howl and Other Poems* by Allen Ginsberg. Copyright

© 1956, 1959 by Allen Ginsberg. "First Party at Ken Kesey's with the Hell's Angels"; from "Wichita Vortex Sutra," page 122–page 126; and, "Wales Visitation," from *Planet News* by Allen Ginsberg. Copyright © 1968 by Allen Ginsberg. Reprinted by permission of City Lights Books.

Robert Hayden, "Middle Passage," from *Selected Poems* by Robert Hayden. Copyright © 1966 by Robert Hayden. Reprinted by permission of October House Inc.

Randall Jarrell, "Come to the Stone"; "The Death of the Ball Turret Gunner"; and, "The Sick Nought," from *The Complete Poems* by Randall Jarrell. Copyright © 1943, 1944, 1945, 1969 by Mrs. Randall Jarrell, copyright renewed 1970, 1971 by Mrs. Randall Jarrell. Reprinted by permission of Farrar, Straus & Giroux, Inc.

Bob Kaufman, "Plea," from *Golden Sardine* by Bob Kaufman. Copyright © 1967 by Bob Kaufman. Reprinted by permission of City Lights Books. "Jail Poems," from *Solitudes Crowded with Loneliness* by Bob Kaufman. Copyright © 1959–1965 by Bob Kaufman. Reprinted by permission of New Directions Publishing Corporation.

Weldon Kees, "For My Daughter"; "White Collar Ballad"; and, "Robinson," from *The Collected Poems of Weldon Kees*. Copyright © by University of Nebraska Press. Reprinted by permission of University of Nebraska Press.

Kenneth Koch, "Fresh Air," from *Thank You and Other Poems* by Kenneth Koch. Copyright © 1962 by Kenneth Koch. Reprinted by permission of Grove Press, Inc.

Don L. Lee, "In a Period of Growth," from *Think Black* by Don L. Lee. Copyright © by Broadside Press. "Assassination," and, "The Revolutionary Screw," from *Don't Cry, Scream* by Don L. Lee. Copyright © by Broadside Press. Reprinted by permission of Broadside Press.

Denise Levertov, "Hypocrite Women," from *O Taste and See* by Denise Levertov. Copyright © 1963, 1964 by Denise Levertov Goodman. "What Were They Like?" from *The Sorrow Dance* by Denise Levertov. Copyright © 1966 by Denise Levertov Goodman. Reprinted by permission of New Directions Publishing Corporation.

Robert Lowell, "Children of Light," from *Lord Weary's Castle* by Robert Lowell. Copyright © 1946 by Robert Lowell. Reprinted by permission of Harcourt, Brace, Jovanovich, Inc. "Memories of West Street and Lepke," from *Life Studies* by Robert Lowell. Copyright © 1958 by Robert Lowell. "The Mouth of the Hudson" and, "For the Union Dead," from *For the Union Dead* by Robert Lowell. Copyright © 1960, 1964 by Robert Lowell. Reprinted by permission of Farrar, Straus & Giroux, Inc.

W. S. Merwin, "Air," from *The Moving Target* by W. S. Merwin. Copyright © 1962 by W. S. Merwin. Reprinted by permission of Atheneum Publishers. Appeared originally in *Poetry*. "In One of the Retreats of Morning," from *The Lice* by W. S. Merwin. Copyright © 1967 by W. S. Merwin. Reprinted by permission of Atheneum Publishers.

Josephine Miles, "Ride" and, "Autumnal," from *Prefabrications* by Josephine Miles. Copyright © 1955 by Josephine Miles. Reprinted by permission of Indiana University Press. "Yesterday Evening as the Sun Set Late." Copyright © 1967 by Josephine Miles. Reprinted from *Kinds of Affection*, by Josephine Miles. Reprinted by permission of Wesleyan University Press.

Marianne Moore, "Poetry," from *Collected Poems* by Marianne Moore. Copyright © 1935 by Marianne Moore, renewed 1963 by Marianne Moore and T. S. Eliot. Reprinted with permission of The Macmillan Company.

Frank O'Hara, "Steps," from *Lunch Poems* by Frank O'Hara. Copyright © 1964 by Frank O'Hara. Reprinted by permission of City Lights Books.

Charles Olson, "Song 1" and "Song 3" from *The Maximus Poems* by Charles Olson. Copyright © by Charles Olson. Reprinted by permission of Corinth Books. "There Was a Youth Whose Name Was Thomas Granger," from *The Distances* by Charles Olson. Copyright © 1950, 1951, 1953, 1960 by Charles Olson. Reprinted by permission of Grove Press, Inc.

Sylvia Plath, "All the Dead Dears"; "The Disquieting Muses"; "Night Shift"; and, "The Colossus," from *The Colossus and Other Poems* by Sylvia Plath. Copyright © 1962 by Sylvia Plath. Reprinted by permission of Alfred A. Knopf, Inc. "You're," from *Ariel* by Sylvia Plath. Copyright © 1961 by Ted Hughes. "Tulips," from *Ariel* by Sylvia Plath. Copyright © 1962 by Ted Hughes. "Lady Lazarus"; "Daddy"; and, "Edge," from *Ariel* by Sylvia Plath. Copyright © 1963 by Ted Hughes. "Ariel" and, "Words," from *Ariel* by Sylvia Plath. Copyright © 1965 by Ted Hughes. Reprinted by permission of Harper & Row, Publishers, Inc.

Ezra Pound, "The River-Merchant's Wife: A Letter"; "In a Station of the Metro"; "Lament of the Frontier Guard"; "Salutation"; "The Rest"; and, "Alba from 'Langue d'Oc'," from *Personae* by Ezra Pound. Copyright © 1926 by Ezra Pound. Reprinted by permission of New Directions Publishing Corporation. "Canto XLV," from *The Cantos* by Ezra Pound. Copyright © 1937 by Ezra Pound. Reprinted by permission of New Directions Publishing Corporation.

Ishmael Reed, "I Am a Cowboy in the Boat of Ra." Copyright © 1968, 1969, 1970 by Ishmael Reed. Reprinted by permission of the author.

Otis Redding, "(Sittin' on) The Dock of the Bay," by Steve Cropper and Otis Redding. Copyright © 1968, 1969 by East/Memphis Music Corp., Redwal Music Co., Inc., and Time Music Co., Inc. All rights administered by East/Memphis Music Corp., 926 E. McLemore Ave., Memphis, Tenn. 38106. All rights reserved. International Copyright secured.

Adrienne Rich, "After Dark," from *Necessities of Life* by Adrienne Rich. Copyright © 1966 by W. W. Norton & Company, Inc. Reprinted by permission of W. W. Norton & Company, Inc.

Theodore Roethke, "Dolor," from *Collected Poems of Theodore Roethke*. Copyright © 1943 by Modern Poetry Association, Inc. Reprinted by permission of Doubleday & Company, Inc. "The Minimal," from *The Collected Poems of Theodore Roethke*. Copyright © 1942 by Theodore Roethke. "The Lost Son," from *The Collected Poems of Theodore Roethke*. Copyright © 1947 by Theodore Roethke. Reprinted by permission of Doubleday & Company, Inc.

Sonia Sanchez, "Malcolm" and, "Poem (for DCs 8th Graders—1966-67)," from *Homecoming* by Sonia Sanchez. Copyright © 1969 by Sonia Sanchez. Reprinted by permission of Broadside Press.

James Schuyler, "With Frank and George at Lexington," copyright © 1964 by "Societe Anonyme 'd Editions Literature Et Artistques," "Poem," copyright © 1968 by The Poetry Project, St. Marks Church-In-The-Bowery, "3/23/66," copyright © 1969 by James Schuyler from the book *Freely Espousing* by James Schuyler. Reprinted by permission of Doubleday & Company, Inc.

Anne Sexton, "Unknown Girl in the Maternity Ward," from *To Bedlam and Part Way Back* by Anne Sexton. Copyright © 1960 by Anne Sexton. "Consorting with Angels" and, "Live," from *Live or Die* by Anne Sexton. Copyright © 1966 by Anne Sexton. Reprinted by permission of the publisher, Houghton Mifflin Company.

Charles Simic, "My Shoes"; "Stone"; "Poem Without a Title" and, "Stone Inside a Stone," George Braziller, Inc.—from *Dismantling the Silence* by Charles Simic. Copyright © 1971 by Charles Simic. Reprinted by permission of the publisher.

Grace Slick, "White Rabbit," words and music by Grace Slick. Copyright © 1966 by Copperpenny Music Publishing Company, Inc. and Irving Music, Inc. (BMI). Reprinted by permission of Irving Music, Inc.

Gary Snyder, "For a Far-out Friend"; "Marin-An"; "Mid-August at Sourdough Mountain Lookout"; and, "Hay for the Horses," from *The Back Country* by Gary Snyder. Copyright © 1968 by Gary Snyder. Reprinted by permission of New Directions Publishing Corporation. "Bubbs Creek Haircut," from *Six Sections from Mountain and Rivers Without End* by Gary Snyder. Copyright © 1961 by Gary Snyder. Reprinted by permission. "Revolution in the Revolution in the Revolution"; "What You Should Know to be a Poet"; "Wave," first published in *Poetry* by Gary Snyder; "Song of the Taste," first published in *Poetry* and, "Long Hair," from *Regarding Wave* by Gary Snyder. Copyright © 1968, 1970 by Gary Snyder. Reprinted by permission of New Directions Publishing Corporation.

William Stafford, "Traveling Through the Dark," from *Traveling Through the Dark* by William Stafford. Copyright © 1960 by William Stafford. Reprinted by permission of Harper & Row, Publishers, Inc.

Diane Wakoski, "Reaching Out with the Hands of the Sun," from *The Magellanic Clouds* published by Black Sparrow Press, P.O. Box 25603, Los Angeles, Calif. 90025. Copyright © 1970 by Diane Wakoski. Reprinted by permission of Black Sparrow Press.

James Welch, "Getting Things Straight," from *Hearse #14*. Copyright © 1970 by Hearse Press. Reprinted by permission of Hearse Press. "Harlem, Montana: Just Off the Reservation," from *Riding the Earthboy 40* by James Welch. Copyright © 1971 by James Welch. First published in *Poetry*. Reprinted by permission of The World Publishing Company.

Jonathan Williams, "From Uncle Jack Carpenter's Anthology of Death on Three-Mile Creek"; "The Epitaph on Uncle Nick Grindstaff's Grave on the Iron Mountain Above Shady Valley, Tennessee"; and, "Paint Sign on a Rough Rock Yonside of Boone Side of Shady Valley," from *An Ear in Bartram's Tree* by Jonathan Williams. Copyright © by Jonathan Williams. Reprinted by permission of University of North Carolina Press.

William Carlos Williams, "This Is Just to Say"; "A Bastard Peace"; "Apology"; "Love Song"; "To a Poor Old Woman"; and, "The Last Words of My English Grandmother," from *Collected Earlier Poems* by William Carlos Williams. Copyright © 1938 by William Carlos Williams. Reprinted by permission of New Directions Publishing Corporation.

James Wright, "A Blessing"; "Autumn Begins in Martins Ferry, Ohio" and, "Stages on a Journey Westward," from *The Branch Will Not Break* by James Wright. Copyright © 1961, 1962, 1963 by James Wright. Reprinted by permission of Wesleyan University Press.

CONTENTS

INTRODUCTION   *1*
WILLIAM CARLOS WILLIAMS
  This Is Just to Say   *7*
  A Bastard Peace   *8*
  Apology   *9*
  Love Song   *10*
  To a Poor Old Woman   *10*
  The Last Words of My English Grandmother   *11*
EZRA POUND
  The River-Merchant's Wife: A Letter   *13*
  In a Station of the Metro   *14*
  Lament of the Frontier Guard   *14*
  Salutation   *15*
  The Rest   *15*
  Alba from "Langue d'Oc"   *16*
  Canto XLV   *17*
MARIANNE MOORE
  Poetry   *19*
BESSIE SMITH
  Young Woman's Blues   *21*
E. E. CUMMINGS
  Since Feeling Is First   *23*
  I Sing of Olaf Glad and Big   *23*
THEODORE ROETHKE
  Dolor   *25*
  The Minimal   *25*
  The Lost Son   *26*
CHARLES OLSON
  from The Songs of Maximus   *31*
  There Was a Youth Whose Name Was Thomas Granger   *33*

JOSEPHINE MILES
  Ride   *36*
  Autumnal   *36*
  Yesterday Evening as the Sun Set Late   *37*

WOODY GUTHRIE
  This Land Is Your Land   *39*
  Pastures of Plenty   *40*
  Plane Wreck at Los Gatos (Deportee) (Goodbye, Juan)   *41*
  Mail Myself to You   *42*

ROBERT HAYDEN
  Middle Passage   *44*

WELDON KEES
  For My Daughter   *50*
  White Collar Ballad   *51*
  Robinson   *51*

WILLIAM STAFFORD
  Traveling Through the Dark   *53*

RANDALL JARRELL
  Come to the Stone . . .   *54*
  The Death of the Ball Turret Gunner   *55*
  The Sick Nought   *55*

GWENDOLYN BROOKS
  Sadie and Maud   *56*
  Jessie Mitchell's Mother   *57*
  We Real Cool   *57*
  from The Womanhood (section VIII)
    Beverly Hills, Chicago   *58*

ROBERT LOWELL
  Children of Light   *60*
  Memories of West Street and Lepke   *61*
  The Mouth of the Hudson   *62*
  For the Union Dead   *63*

LAWRENCE FERLINGHETTI
  In Goya's Greatest Scenes We Seem to See   *66*
  After the Cries of the Birds   *67*

PETE SEEGER
  Where Have All the Flowers Gone?   *73*

ROBERT DUNCAN
  Nel Mezzo del Cammin di Nostra Vita   75
  The Multiversity   Passages 21   78

JAMES DICKEY
  Cherrylog Road   81

DENISE LEVERTOV
  Hypocrite Women   85
  What Were They Like?   86

JAMES SCHUYLER
  With Frank and George at Lexington   87
  Poem   88
  3/23/66   88

EDWARD FIELD
  Graffiti   89
  Unwanted   90
  Frankenstein   91
  The Bride of Frankenstein   92
  The Return of Frankenstein   94

KENNETH KOCH
  Fresh Air   96

BOB KAUFMAN
  Plea   102
  Jail Poems   103

ALLEN GINSBERG
  A Supermarket in California   109
  Sunflower Sutra   112
  America   113
  First Party at Ken Kesey's with the Hell's Angels   116
  from Wichita Vortex Sutra   117
  Wales Visitation   120

FRANK O'HARA
  Steps   123

ROBERT CREELEY
  If You   125
  Oh No   126
  The Rhythm   126
  I Know a Man   127
  Anger   127

xiii

ROBERT BLY
- Driving Toward the Lac Qui Parle River   132
- Ode to My Socks *(Pablo Neruda)*   133
- Looking into a Face   135
- Come with Me   135
- Hatred of Men with Black Hair   136
- Counting Small-Boned Bodies   136
- Sleet Storm on the Merritt Parkway   137
- from The Teeth-Mother Naked at Last   137

JAMES WRIGHT
- A Blessing   141
- Autumn Begins in Martins Ferry, Ohio   142
- Stages on a Journey Westward   142

W. S. MERWIN
- Air   144
- In One of the Retreats of Morning   145

ANNE SEXTON
- Unknown Girl in the Maternity Ward   146
- Consorting with Angels   147
- Live   149

JONATHAN WILLIAMS
- From Uncle Jake Carpenter's Anthology of Death on Three-Mile Creek   153
- The Epitaph on Uncle Nick Grindstaff's Grave on the Iron Mountain above Shady Valley, Tennessee   153
- Paint Sign on a Rough Rock Yonside of Boone Side of Shady Valley   153

ADRIENNE RICH
- After Dark   154

GREGORY CORSO
- Last Night I Drove a Car   157
- Sun   157
- Friend   158
- Marriage   159

GARY SNYDER
- For a Far-out Friend   166
- Marin-An   167
- Mid-August at Sourdough Mountain Lookout   167
- Hay for the Horses   168

Bubbs Creek Haircut   *168*
  What You Should Know to be a Poet   *173*
  Wave   *174*
  Song of the Taste   *175*
  Revolution in the Revolution in the Revolution   *176*
  Long Hair   *176*

SYLVIA PLATH
  All the Dead Dears   *182*
  The Disquieting Muses   *183*
  Night Shift   *185*
  The Colossus   *185*
  You're   *186*
  Tulips   *187*
  Ariel   *189*
  Lady Lazarus   *190*
  Daddy   *193*
  Edge   *195*
  Words   *196*

SAM COOKE
  A Change Is Gonna Come   *198*
  Change Gonna Come *(Otis Redding)*   *199*

IMAMU AMIRI BARAKA (LE ROI JONES)
  I Substitute for the Dead Lecturer   *200*
  A Poem Some People Will Have to Understand   *201*
  Red Light   *202*
  Poem for Halfwhite College Students   *202*
  Loku   *203*
  American Ecstasy   *203*

CHUCK BERRY
  Too Much Monkey Business   *204*
  Roll Over, Beethoven   *206*

ZEL SANDERS AND LONA STEVENS
  Sally, Go 'Round the Roses   *208*

SONIA SANCHEZ
  Malcolm   *209*
  Poem (for DCs 8th Graders—1966-67)   *210*

LUCILLE CLIFTON
  In the Inner City   *211*
  Good Times   *211*

    Ca'line's Prayer   *212*
    For deLawd   *212*
    Admonitions   *213*

DIANE WAKOSKI
    Reaching Out with the Hands of the Sun   *214*

ISHMAEL REED
    I Am a Cowboy in the Boat of Ra   *218*

CHARLES SIMIC
    My Shoes   *221*
    Stone   *221*
    Poem Without a Title   *222*
    Stone Inside a Stone   *222*

FLORENCE ELON
    Visiting Hours   *224*
    Berlin: the Ruined Countess   *225*

JAMES WELCH
    Getting Things Straight   *226*
    Harlem, Montana: Just Off the Reservation   *227*

GRACE SLICK
    White Rabbit   *228*

OTIS REDDING
    The Dock of the Bay   *230*

BOB DYLAN
    Blowin' in the Wind   *233*
    It Ain't Me, Babe   *238*
    Subterranean Homesick Blues   *239*
    Mr. Tambourine Man   *240*
    Lay, Lady, Lay   *242*
    If Dogs Run Free   *243*

PAUL SIMON
    The Sound of Silence   *244*

DON L. LEE
    In a Period of Growth   *246*
    Assassination   *247*
    The Revolutionary Screw   *247*

JOHN BALABAN
    The Guard at the Binh Thuy Bridge   *249*

JIM MORRISON
   The End   *250*

VICTOR HERNÁNDEZ CRUZ
   & Stuff Like That   *252*
   Is a Dead Man   *253*
   Latin & Soul   *255*

PREFACE

Making It New grew out of our interests and concerns with introducing contemporary poetry to students with little or no background in experiencing poetry. In making our selections, we have therefore been guided more by what we feel teaches poetry than what we feel introduces poetry within a literary history or critical theory.

We have chosen examples of recognized poetry, and we have also looked for truly popular poetry—poetry loved and remembered by millions of people. The popular songs in the collection are examples of such a poetry. We have also chosen, wherever we could, poems of social and political importance.

We have organized this book in a simple way, chronologically by date of the writer's birth, but we have not tried to divide the poems into time periods. Major events of the century, though, have a way of getting into poems: the First World War, the Depression, the Second World War, the civil rights movement; and these events and the reactions to them (the soporific, affluent 'fifties following the Second World War, for example) provide a rough framework for the book.

Many other anthologies have been useful to us, among them Donald M. Allen's collection of *The New American Poetry,* 1945-1960 (1960) and *Naked Poetry,* edited by Stephen Berg and Robert Mezey (1969). The best anthologies (and these two are among the best) compromise skillfully between the extremes of many poems from a few poets and a few poems from many poets. Our resolution of this dilemma has been to include a fairly large number of poems from the work of four poets: Allen Ginsberg, Gary Snyder, Sylvia Plath, and Bob Dylan. Each of these four has written prolifically, each is widely admired, and each has developed in an interesting way—Ginsberg and Snyder by working consistently and faithfully with a single body of principles and techniques, Sylvia Plath and Bob Dylan by registering dynamic and dramatic changes in style.

July 1972   J.E.C.
Palo Alto, California   W.M.C.

Making It New

INTRODUCTION

The word "anthology" comes from two Greek words, one meaning "flower" and the other "a gathering." The word implies both variety and excellence. Whoever assembles an anthology chooses poems that to him represent several kinds of the best poetry.

Our selection has been guided by the spirit of Walt Whitman, America's most original poet, and by the spirit of Ezra Pound, whose exhortation to young poets—"MAKE IT NEW"—suggests our title.

Whitman (1819-1892) represents many qualities of the kind of poetry we admire: freedom of form, language, and subject; personal openness and candor; love of the simplicity of ordinary speech; and a passionate interest in contemporary life. A carpenter, printer, journalist, and editor, he printed his own first book of poems in 1855, making them ready for sale on the Fourth of July, a date he chose for its association with American democracy, independence, and revolution. Entitled *Leaves of Grass,* the poems were original. They had long, uneven lines, didn't rhyme, and weren't divided into regular stanzas. To some they would seem formless and undisciplined; to their creator they were as "unerringly" shaped as roses or "leaves of grass."* Among his original ideas Whitman held the belief that poetry could be a kind of opera without music—and in fact often called his poems "songs."

To his contemporaries, the content of the poems was shocking. When *Leaves of Grass* first appeared, a leading American poet was Henry Wadsworth Longfellow. Longfellow wrote poems on subjects from the distant past—Longfellow's *Evangeline* (1847), for example, described the sufferings of French settlers in Canada persecuted for their religion; in *The Song of Hiawatha* (1855) he told of the loves and adventures of a mythical Indian brave. Whitman's longest poem, in contrast, was called "Song of Myself," and he spoke of city streets and crowds, of his body's erotic desires, of his equality with all men, and of his

---

*Preface to the 1855 Edition of *Leaves of Grass.* See, for instance, *The American Tradition in Literature,* "Shorter Edition in One Volume," ed. Sculley Bradley, Richmond Croom Beatty, and E. Hudson Long (New York: W. W. Norton, 1967), p. 891.

own spiritual vastness. The poem was contemporary, humorous, erotic, political, and yet religious; its language varied from common speech to words like "compassionating" and "impalpable."

The direction "Make it new"—from which derives the title of this anthology—comes from Confucius, the Chinese philosopher, statesman, and teacher (551–479 B.C.), by way of Ezra Pound, poet and teacher.*

> Tching prayed on the mountain and
>   wrote MAKE IT NEW
> on his bath tub
>   Day by day make it new
> cut underbrush,
> pile the logs
> keep it growing.

To Pound, who used the words as the title of a collection of essays,* "Make it new" was a kind of motto, both a declaration of purpose and a challenge. "Literature is news that *stays* news," he writes in another place.* The challenge for the poet is double. He must find a language that seems fresh and new, and he must have something of permanent interest to say. Either task alone is greatly difficult. How many of us speak in a way that sounds "new"? Or say anything worth remembering as long as a week?

Like Whitman, Pound also stands for many qualities we admire: a desire to find new forms for poetry, to innovate, to renovate, to keep poetry a living art; a powerful belief in the importance of verbal art; a passionate interest in poetic technique; and a serious interest in social and political life.

Pound aimed to be a great poet, although in his old age (his eighties) he grew unsure of the wisdom of his will to greatness. "I have brought the great ball of crystal," he wrote of his work, "Who can lift it?"* To prepare himself to be a poet, he learned languages: Greek, Latin, some classical Chinese, Old French (Provencal), French, and Italian. He worked at translation, aiming to learn what could be said in poetry in one language only, and what could be said in others. He practiced vigorously: in one youthful year, it is said, he wrote a sonnet a day and threw away all he wrote. Pound also worked socially for poetry, using the kind of energy that one associates with solo flights across

---

*Canto LIII, *The Cantos* (1–95) (New York: New Directions, 1968).

Make It New is the title of a collection of essays by Pound (London: Faber and Faber, 1934).

**ABC of Reading* (New York: New Directions, 1960), p. 29.

*Canto 116, *Ezra Pound Drafts & Fragments of Cantos 110–117* (New York: New Directions, 1968).

the Atlantic or the engineering of the Golden Gate Bridge. He looked for poets (and other artists) of genius. He helped them find patrons. He contributed to magazines with names like *The New Age, Blast, Furioso,* and *To-day.* He worked tirelessly to put before the public the work of the living artists he respected. He edited his friends' work, if they were willing, and sometimes even when they were not.

As members of a troubled society, we want to encourage the reading of poetry that makes direct statements about society and politics. As readers of poetry we admire both Whitman and Pound. In politics, Whitman was a democrat, Pound an elitist. Pound might have gone to hospitals, as Whitman did, to comfort the wounded soldiers—if those soldiers had been artists, and very good ones. The more the poet loves the common people, Whitman might have said, the better his poems will be. Pound is a kind of living symbol for perfection of one's art, and Whitman a symbol of lived art. That is, for Whitman, a poet's life is a kind of poetry, and his art is a process, a record of his living.

Amongst democratic nations, each new generation is a new people. Amongst such nations, then, literature will not easily be subjected to strict rules, and it is impossible that any such rules should ever be permanent.

—ALEXIS DE TOCQUEVILLE, FRENCHMAN, ARISTOCRAT, TRAVELER; *Democracy in America,* 1835, 1840

Perfect poems show the free growth of metrical laws and bud from them as unerringly and loosely as lilacs or roses on a bush, and take shapes as compact as the shapes of chestnuts and oranges.

—WALT WHITMAN, CARPENTER, JOURNALIST, POET; PREFACE TO *Leaves of Grass,* 1855

Music begins to atrophy when it departs too far from the dance; . . . poetry begins to atrophy when it gets too far from music.

—EZRA POUND, POET, CRITIC; *ABC of Reading,* 1934

THIS IS JUST TO SAY

I have eaten
the plums
that were in
the icebox

and which
you were probably
saving
for breakfast

Forgive me
they were delicious
so sweet
and so cold

  —William Carlos Williams

WILLIAM CARLOS WILLIAMS

William Carlos Williams (1883, Rutherford, New Jersey—1963, Rutherford, New Jersey; attended the University of Pennsylvania and the University of Leipzig, Germany) was a doctor (obstetrics, pediatrics, and something of a general practice) as well as a poet. He has authored more than 25 volumes of fiction, poetry, and essays, and has influenced many poets with his theories about the importance of following the natural rhythm of American speech. The poems are from *The Collected Earlier Poems: Before Nineteen Forty* (1951).

He has described poetry thus:

A local pride; spring, summer, fall and the sea; a confession; a basket; a column; a reply to Greek and Latin with the bare hands; a gathering up; a celebration.

—*Epigraph to* Paterson, *a long poem about man and a city*

Of writing poems he says:
To make a start,
out of particulars
and make them general, rolling
up the sum, by defective means—

—*Preface to* Paterson

A BASTARD PEACE

　　　—where a heavy
woven-wire fence
topped with jagged ends, encloses
a long cinder-field by the river—

A concrete disposal tank at
one end, small wooden
pit-covers scattered about—above
sewer intakes, most probably—

Down the center's a service path
graced on one side by
a dandelion in bloom—and a white
butterfly—

The sun parches still
the parched grass. Along
the fence, blocked from the water
leans the washed-out street—

Three cracked houses—
a willow, two chickens, a
small boy, with a home-made push cart,
walking by, waving a whip—

Gid ap! No other traffic or
like to be.
There to rest, to improvise and
unbend! Through the fence

beyond the field and shining
water, 12 o'clock blows
but nobody goes
other than the kids from school—

APOLOGY

Why do I write today?

The beauty of
the terrible faces
of our nonentities
stirs me to it:

colored women
day workers—
old and experienced—
returning home at dusk
in cast off clothing
faces like
old Florentine oak.

Also

the set pieces
of your faces stir me—
leading citizens—
but not
in the same way.

LOVE SONG

Sweep the house clean,
hang fresh curtains
in the windows
put on a new dress
and come with me!
The elm is scattering
its little loaves
of sweet smells
from a white sky!

Who shall hear of us
in the time to come?
Let him say there was
a burst of fragrance
from black branches.

TO A POOR OLD WOMAN

munching a plum on
the street a paper bag
of them in her hand

They taste good to her
They taste good
to her. They taste
good to her

You can see it by
the way she gives herself
to the one half
sucked out in her hand

Comforted
a solace of ripe plums
seeming to fill the air
They taste good to her

THE LAST WORDS OF MY ENGLISH GRANDMOTHER

There were some dirty plates
and a glass of milk
beside her on a small table
near the rank, disheveled bed—

Wrinkled and nearly blind
she lay and snored
rousing with anger in her tones
to cry for food,

Gimme something to eat—
They're starving me—
I'm all right I won't go
to the hospital. No, no, no

Give me something to eat
Let me take you
to the hospital, I said
and after you are well

you can do as you please.
She smiled, Yes
you do what you please first
then I can do what I please—

Oh, oh, oh! she cried
as the ambulance men lifted
her to the stretcher—
Is this what you call

making me comfortable?
By now her mind was clear—
Oh you think you're smart
you young people,

she said, but I'll tell you
you don't know anything.
Then we started.
On the way

we passed a long row
of elms. She looked at them
awhile out of
the ambulance window and said,

What are all those
fuzzy-looking things out there?
Trees? Well, I'm tired
of them and rolled her head away.

EZRA POUND

Ezra Weston Loomis Pound was born in 1885 in Hailey, Idaho. He attended Hamilton College and the University of Pennsylvania, and he died in Venice, Italy, in 1972. The Anglo-American poet W. H. Auden once said, "There are few living poets, even if they are not conscious of having been influenced by Pound, who would say, 'My work would be exactly the same if Mr. Pound had never lived.'" T. S. Eliot, speaking of Pound's stunning translations from the Chinese, called him "the inventor of Chinese poetry for our time." Eliot's *The Waste Land* was brilliantly edited by Pound.

Pound has written a long historical and prophetic poem called *The Cantos*. These poems come from *Selected Poems of Ezra Pound* (1957).

THE RIVER-MERCHANT'S WIFE: A LETTER

While my hair was still cut straight across my forehead
Played I about the front gate, pulling flowers.
You came by on bamboo stilts, playing horse,
You walked about my seat, playing with blue plums.
And we went on living in the village of Chokan:
Two small people, without dislike or suspicion.

At fourteen I married My Lord you.
I never laughed, being bashful.
Lowering my head, I looked at the wall.
Called to, a thousand times, I never looked back.

At fifteen I stopped scowling,
I desired my dust to be mingled with yours
Forever and forever and forever.
Why should I climb the look out?

At sixteen you departed,
You went into far Ku-to-yen, by the river of swirling eddies,
And you have been gone five months.
The monkeys make sorrowful noise overhead.

You dragged your feet when you went out.
By the gate now, the moss is grown, the different mosses,
Too deep to clear them away!
The leaves fall early this autumn, in wind.
The paired butterflies are already yellow with August
Over the grass in the West garden;
They hurt me. I grow older.
If you are coming down through the narrows of the river
    Kiang,
Please let me know beforehand,
And I will come out to meet you
        As far as Cho-fu-Sa.

By Rihaku

IN A STATION OF THE METRO[1]

The apparition of these faces in the crowd;
Petals on a wet, black bough.

   [1] *the metro* the subway system in Paris.

LAMENT OF THE FRONTIER GUARD

By the North Gate, the wind blows full of sand,
Lonely from the beginning of time until now!
Trees fall, the grass goes yellow with autumn.
I climb the towers and towers
      to watch out the barbarous land:
Desolate castle, the sky, the wide desert.
There is no wall left to this village.
Bones white with a thousand frosts,
High heaps, covered with trees and grass;
Who brought this to pass?
Who has brought the flaming imperial anger?
Who has brought the army with drums and with kettle-drums?
Barbarous kings.
A gracious spring, turned to blood-ravenous autumn,
A turmoil of wars-men, spread over the middle kingdom,
Three hundred and sixty thousand,
And sorrow, sorrow like rain.
Sorrow to go, and sorrow, sorrow returning.

Desolate, desolate fields,
And no children of warfare upon them,
    No longer the men for offence and defence.
Ah, how shall you know the dreary sorrow at the North Gate,
With Rihoku's name forgotten,
And we guardsmen fed to the tigers.

By Rihaku

SALUTATION

O generation of the thoroughly smug
    and thoroughly uncomfortable,
I have seen fishermen picnicking in the sun,
I have seen them with untidy families,
I have seen their smiles full of teeth
    and heard ungainly laughter.
And I am happier than you are,
And they were happier than I am;
And the fish swim in the lake
    and do not even own clothing.

THE REST

O helpless few in my country,
O remnant enslaved!

Artists broken against her,
A-stray, lost in the villages,
Mistrusted, spoken-against,

Lovers of beauty, starved,
Thwarted with systems,
Helpless against the control;

You who can not wear yourselves out
By persisting to successes,
You who can only speak,
Who can not steel yourselves into reiteration;

You of the finer sense,
Broken against false knowledge,
You who can know at first hand,
Hated, shut in, mistrusted:

Take thought:
I have weathered the storm,
I have beaten out my exile.

ALBA[1]

from "Langue d'Oc"[2]

When the nightingale to his mate
Sings day-long and night late
My love and I keep state
In bower,
In flower,
'Till the watchman on the tower
Cry:
        "Up! Thou rascal, Rise,
        I see the white
           Light
           And the night
              Flies."

[1]*alba* a dawn-song, more specifically, a song sung by a friend to warn a lover that dawn is breaking and that he must leave his lady. [2]*Langue d'Oc* Provençal, the language of Southern France in which the word for "yes" was "oc" not "oui."

CANTO XLV

With *Usura*[1]
With usura hath no man a house of good stone
each block cut smooth and well fitting
that design might cover their face,
with usura
hath no man a painted paradise on his church wall
harpes et luthes[2]
or where virgin receiveth message
and halo projects from incision,
with usura
seeth no man Gonzaga his heirs and his concubines
no picture is made to endure nor to live with
but it is made to sell and sell quickly
with usura, sin against nature,
is thy bread dry as paper,
is thy bread dry as paper,
with no mountain wheat, no strong flour
with usura the line grows thick
with usura is no clear demarcation
and no man can find site for his dwelling.
Stone cutter is kept from his stone
weaver is kept from his loom

WITH USURA
wool comes not to market
sheep bringeth no gain with usura
Usura is a murrain, usura
blunteth the needle in the maid's hand
and stoppeth the spinner's cunning. Pietro Lombardo[3]
came not by usura
Duccio came not by usura
nor Pier della Francesca; Zuan Bellin' not by usura
nor was 'La Calunnia' painted.
Came not by usura Angelico; came not Ambrogio Praedis,
Came no church of cut stone signed: *Adamo me fecit.*[4]
Not by usura St Trophime
Not by usura Saint Hilaire,
Usura rusteth the chisel
It rusteth the craft and the craftsman
It gnaweth the thread in the loom
None learneth to weave gold in her pattern;

Azure hath a canker by usura; cramoisi is unbroidered
Emerald findeth no Memling
Usura slayeth the child in the womb
It stayeth the young man's courting
It hath brought palsey to bed, lyeth
between the young bride and her bridegroom
      CONTRA NATURAM[5]
They have brought whores for Eleusis[6]
Corpses are set to banquet
at behest of usura.

 [1]*Usura* usury, the charging of interest on money loaned. During the Middle Ages the Church made this activity a heavy sin. [2]*Harpes et luthes* "harps and lutes." [3]The proper names are artists and works of art known from the Middle Ages and early Renaissance. [4]*Adamo me fecit* "Adam made me." [5]*contra naturam* "against nature." [6]*Eleusis* a Greek town where religious rites of spring were celebrated.

MARIANNE MOORE

Marianne Moore was born in 1887 in Kirkwood, Missouri (near St. Louis), and died in 1972 in New York City. She attended Bryn Mawr College. In 1951 *The Collected Poems of Marianne Moore* won three chief awards for poetry: the Bollingen Prize, the National Book Award, and the Pulitzer Prize. She has been a teacher of commercial subjects, a librarian, and an editor on the staff of *The Dial,* a very distinguished magazine of the twenties. For many years Miss Moore was a resident of Brooklyn, New York, and a vigorous supporter of the baseball team of that borough. She has translated the *Fables* of La Fontaine.

"Poetry" comes from *The Collected Poems* (1951).

POETRY

I, too, dislike it: there are things that are important beyond all this fiddle.
    Reading it, however, with a perfect contempt for it, one discovers in
        it after all, a place for the genuine.
            Hands that can grasp, eyes
            that can dilate, hair that can rise
                if it must, these things are important not because a

high-sounding interpretation can be put upon them but because they are
    useful. When they become so derivative as to become unintelligible,
        the same thing may be said for all of us, that we
            do not admire what
            we cannot understand: the bat
                holding on upside down or in quest of something to

eat, elephants pushing, a wild horse taking a roll, a tireless wolf under
    a tree, the immovable critic twitching his skin like a horse that
        feels a flea, the base-
ball fan, the statistician—
        nor is it valid
            to discriminate against 'business documents and

school-books'; all these phenomena are important. One must make a
    distinction
  however: when dragged into prominence by half poets, the result
    is not poetry,
  nor till the poets among us can be
    'literalists of
    the imagination'—above
      insolence and triviality and can present

for inspection, 'imaginary gardens with real toads in them,' shall we
    have
  it. In the meantime, if you demand on the one hand,
  the raw material of poetry in
    all its rawness and
    that which is on the other hand
      genuine, you are interested in poetry.

BESSIE SMITH

Blues singer Bessie Smith (born 1895, Chattanooga, Tennessee) earned as much as $2000 a week on the black vaudeville circuit during the 1920s, and her records sold in the millions. She died in 1937 as the result of an automobile accident.

Bessie Smith wrote "Young Woman's Blues," and may have improvised additions to J. C. Johnson's "Empty Bed Blues." "Young Woman's Blues," recorded in 1926, is on *The Bessie Smith Story*, Vol. 3, (Columbia LP GL 505). "Empty Bed Blues," recorded in 1928, is on *The Bessie Smith Story*, Vol. 4, (Columbia LP CL 858).

YOUNG WOMAN'S BLUES*

Woke up this mornin'
When chickens were crowin' for day.
And on the right side of my pillow,
My man had gone away.
By his pillow he left a note
Readin', "I'm sorry, Jane, you got my goat,
No time to marry, no time to settle down."
I'm a young woman and ain't done runnin' round.
Some people call me a hobo, some call me a bum,
Nobody knows my name, nobody knows what I've done.
I'm as good as any woman in your town.
I ain't no high yella, I'm a deep yella brown.
I ain't gonna marry
Ain't gonna settle down,
I'm gonna drink good moonshine
And run these browns down.
See that long lonesome road?
Don't you know it's gotta end?
And I'm a good woman,
And I can get plenty men.

* © copyright 1927, 1955 Empress Music Inc. Used by permission of the Publisher. All rights reserved.

E. E. CUMMINGS

Edward Estlin Cummings was born in 1894 in Cambridge, Massachusetts, and died in 1963. During World War I he served in a volunteer ambulance corps. After the war he lived in France. Cummings was a painter as well as a poet. His father was a minister in Boston and a teacher at Harvard, where Cummings went to school. The poems come from *is 5* (1926) and *Poems 1923–1954* (1959).

SINCE FEELING IS FIRST

since feeling is first
who pays any attention
to the syntax of things
will never wholly kiss you;

wholly to be a fool
while Spring is in the world

my blood approves,
and kisses are a better fate
than wisdom
lady i swear by all flowers. Don't cry
—the best gesture of my brain is less than
your eyelids' flutter which says

we are for each other: then
laugh, leaning back in my arms
for life's not a paragraph

And death i think is no parenthesis

I SING OF OLAF GLAD AND BIG

i sing of Olaf glad and big
whose warmest heart recoiled at war:
a conscientious object-or

his wellbelovéd colonel (trig
westpointer most succinctly bred)
took erring Olaf soon in hand;
but—though an host of overjoyed
noncoms (first knocking on the head
him) do through icy waters roll
that helplessness which others stroke
with brushes recently employed
anent this muddy toiletbowl,
while kindred intellects evoke
allegiance per blunt instruments—
Olaf (being to all intents
a corpse and wanting any rag
upon what God unto him gave)
responds, without getting annoyed
"I will not kiss your f.ing flag"
straightway the silver bird looked grave
(departing hurriedly to shave)

but—though all kinds of officers
(a yearning nation's blueeyed pride)
their passive prey did kick and curse
until for wear their clarion
voices and boots were much the worse,
and egged the firstclassprivates on
his rectum wickedly to tease
by means of skilfully applied
bayonets roasted hot with heat—
Olaf (upon what were once knees)
does almost ceaselessly repeat
"there is some s. I will not eat"

our president, being of which
assertions duly notified
threw the yellowsonofabitch
into a dungeon, where he died

Christ (of His mercy infinite)
i pray to see; and Olaf, too

preponderatingly because
unless statistics lie he was
more brave than me: more blond than you.

THEODORE ROETHKE

Theodore Roethke was born in 1908 in Saginaw, Michigan. He grew up in Michigan, went to school at the University of Michigan, and taught for many years at the University of Washington, Seattle. His father was a nurseryman and wholesale florist. The "mad" sections of "The Lost Son" may reflect something of what Roethke felt during recurrent nervous breakdowns. He died in Seattle in 1963. The poems are from the *Collected Poems* (1966).

DOLOR

I have known the inexorable sadness of pencils,
Neat in their boxes, dolor of pad and paper-weight,
All the misery of manilla folders and mucilage,
Desolation in immaculate public places,
Lonely reception room, lavatory, switchboard,
The unalterable pathos of basin and pitcher,
Ritual of multigraph, paper-clip, comma,
Endless duplication of lives and objects.
And I have seen dust from the walls of institutions,
Finer than flour, alive, more dangerous than silica,
Sift, almost invisible, through long afternoons of tedium,
Dropping a fine film on nails and delicate eyebrows,
Glazing the pale hair, the duplicate grey standard faces.

THE MINIMAL

I study the lives on a leaf: the little
Sleepers, numb nudgers in cold dimensions,
Beetles in caves, newts, stone-deaf fishes,
Lice tethered to long limp subterranean weeds,
Squirmers in bogs,
And bacterial creepers
Wriggling through wounds
Like elvers in ponds,
Their wan mouths kissing the warm sutures,
Cleaning and caressing,
Creeping and healing.

THE LOST SON

1. The Flight

At Woodlawn I heard the dead cry:
I was lulled by the slamming of iron,
A slow drip over stones,
Toads brooding wells.
All the leaves stuck out their tongues;
I shook the softening chalk of my bones,
Saying,
Snail, snail, glister me forward,
Bird, soft-sigh me home,
Worm, be with me.
This is my hard time.

Fished in an old wound,
The soft pond of repose;
Nothing nibbled my line,
Not even the minnows came.

Sat in an empty house
Watching shadows crawl,
Scratching.
There was one fly.

Voice, come out of the silence.
Say something.
Appear in the form of a spider
Or a moth beating the curtain.

Tell me:
Which is the way I take;
Out of what door do I go,
Where and to whom?

Dark hollows said, lee to the wind,
The moon said, back of an eel,
The salt said, look by the sea,
Your tears are not enough praise,
You will find no comfort here,
In the kingdom of bang and blab.

Running lightly over spongy ground,
Past the pasture of flat stones,
The three elms,
The sheep strewn on a field,
Over a rickety bridge
Toward the quick-water, wrinkling and rippling.

Hunting along the river,
Down among the rubbish, the bug-riddled foliage,
By the muddy pond-edge, by the bog-holes,
By the shrunken lake, hunting, in the heat of summer.

The shape of a rat?
    It's bigger than that.
    It's less than a leg
    And more than a nose,
    Just under the water
    It usually goes.

Is it soft like a mouse?
Can it wrinkle its nose?
Could it come in the house
On the tips of its toes?

    Take the skin of a cat
    And the back of an eel,
    Then roll them in grease,—
    That's the way it would feel.

    It's sleek as an otter
    With wide webby toes
    Just under the water
    It usually goes.

2. The Pit

Where do the roots go?
  Look down under the leaves.
Who put the moss there?
  These stones have been here too long.
Who stunned the dirt into noise?
  Ask the mole, he knows.
I feel the slime of a wet nest.

Beware Mother Mildew.
Nibble again, fish nerves.

3. The Gibber

At the wood's mouth,
By the cave's door,
I listened to something
I had heard before.

Dogs of the groin
Barked and howled,
The sun was against me,
The moon would not have me.

The weeds whined,
The snakes cried,
The cows and briars
Said to me: Die.

What a small song. What slow clouds. What dark water.
Hath the rain a father? All the caves are ice. Only the snow's here.
I'm cold. I'm cold all over. Rub me in father and mother.
Fear was my father, Father Fear.
His look drained the stones.

      What gliding shape
      Beckoning through halls,
      Stood poised on the stair,
      Fell dreamily down?

      From the mouths of jugs
      Perched on many shelves,
      I saw substance flowing
      That cold morning.

      Like a slither of eels
      That watery cheek
      As my own tongue kissed
      My lips awake.

Is this the storm's heart? The ground is unstilling itself.
My veins are running nowhere. Do the bones cast out their fire?
Is the seed leaving the old bed? These buds are live as birds.
Where, where are the tears of the world?

Let the kisses resound, flat like a butcher's palm;
Let the gestures freeze; our doom is already decided.
All the windows are burning! What's left of my life?
I want the old rage, the lash of primordial milk!
Goodbye, goodbye, old stones, the time-order is going,
I have married my hands to perpetual agitation,
I run, I run to the whistle of money.

    Money money money
    Water water water

    How cool the grass is.
    Has the bird left?
    The stalk still sways.
    Has the worm a shadow?
    What do the clouds say?

    These sweeps of light undo me.
    Look, look, the ditch is running white!
    I've more veins than a tree!
    Kiss me, ashes, I'm falling through a dark swirl.

4. The Return

    The way to the boiler was dark,
    Dark all the way,
    Over slippery cinders
    Through the long greenhouse.

    The roses kept breathing in the dark.
    They had many mouths to breathe with.
    My knees made little winds underneath
    Where the weeds slept.

    There was always a single light
    Swinging by the fire-pit,
    Where the fireman pulled out roses,
    The big roses, the big bloody clinkers.

    Once I stayed all night.
    The light in the morning came slowly over the white
    Snow.

    There were many kinds of cool
    Air.
    Then came steam.

>Pipe-knock.

Scurry of warm over small plants.
Ordnung! ordnung!
Papa is coming!

>A fine haze moved off the leaves;
>Frost melted on far panes;
>The rose, the chrysanthemum turned toward the light.
>Even the hushed forms, the bent yellow weeds
>Moved in a slow up-sway.

5. "It was beginning winter"

It was beginning winter,
An in-between time,
The landscape still partly brown:
The bones of weeds kept swinging in the wind,
Above the blue snow.

It was beginning winter,
The light moved slowly over the frozen field,
Over the dry seed-crowns,
The beautiful surviving bones
Swinging in the wind.

Light traveled over the wide field;
Stayed.
The weeds stopped swinging.
The mind moved, not alone,
Through the clear air, in the silence.

>Was it light?
>Was it light within?
>Was it light within light?
>Stillness becoming alive,
>Yet still?

A lively understandable spirit
Once entertained you.
It will come again.
Be still.
Wait.

CHARLES OLSON

Charles Olson was born in Worcester, Massachusetts, in 1910, attended Wesleyan, Yale and Harvard, and taught for a number of years at Black Mountain College in North Carolina. He was a scholar, the author of a work on the sources in Shakespeare of Herman Melville's novel, *Moby Dick*. He was a student of Mayan hieroglyphics and lived for a time in the Yucátan region of Mexico. Two of his students from Black Mountain—Robert Creeley and Robert Duncan —are represented here. Olson was influential as a theorist and as a helpful, practical critic of the verse of others. He died in 1970. The poems are from *The Maximus Poems* (1960) and *The Distances* (1960).

Of poetry he has said:

FORM IS NEVER MORE THAN AN EXTENSION OF CONTENT.

Let's start from the smallest particle of all, the syllable. It is the king and pin of versification, what rules and holds together the lines, the larger forms, of a poem.

It is from the union of the mind and the ear that the syllable is born.

. . . Together, these two, the syllable *and* the line, they make a poem.

And the line comes (I swear it) from the breath, from the breathing of the man who writes, at the moment that he writes.
—"PROJECTIVE VERSE . . . VS. THE NON-PROJECTIVE,"
Poetry New York, NO. 3, 1950

from THE SONGS OF MAXIMUS

Song 1

          colored pictures
of all things to eat: dirty
postcards
       And words, words, words
all over everything
             No eyes or ears left

to do their own doings (all

invaded, appropriated, outraged, all senses

including the mind, that worker on what is
And that other sense
made to give even the most wretched, or any of us, wretched,
that consolation (greased
                        lulled
even the street-cars

song

Song 3
        This morning of the small snow
I count the blessings, the leak in the faucet
which makes of the sink time, the drop
of the water on water as sweet
as the Seth Thomas
in the old kitchen
my father stood in his drawers to wind (always
he forgot the 30th day, as I don't want to remember
the rent
        a house these days
so much somebody else's,
especially,
Congoleum's

        Or the plumbing,
that it doesn't work, this I like, have even used paper clips
as well as string to hold the ball up And flush it
with my hand
        But that the car doesn't, that no moving thing moves
without that song I'd void my ear of, the musickracket
of all ownership . . .
        Holes
in my shoes, that's all right, my fly
gaping, me out
at the elbows, the blessing
that difficulties are once more

"In the midst of plenty, walk
as close to
bare
      In the face of sweetness,
piss
         In the time of goodness,
go side, go
smashing, beat them, go as
(as near as you can

tear

In the land of plenty, have
nothing to do with it
              take the way of
the lowest,
including
your legs, go
contrary, go

sing

THERE WAS A YOUTH
WHOSE NAME WAS THOMAS GRANGER

1

From the beginning, SIN
and the reason, note, known from the start

says Mr. bradford: As it is with waters when
their streames are stopped or damed up, wickednes
(Morton, Morton, Morton)
here by strict laws as in no place more,
or so much, that I have known or heard of,
and ye same more nerly looked unto
(Tom Granger)
so, as it cannot rune in a comone road of liberty
as it would, and is inclined,

it searches every wher (everywhere)
and breaks out wher it getts vente, says he

Rest, Tom, in your pit where they put you
a great & large pitte digged of purposs for them
of Duxbery, servant, being aboute 16. or 17. years of age
his father & mother living at the time at Sityate

espetially drunkennes & unclainnes
incontinencie betweene persons unmaried
but some maried persons allso
And that which is worse
(things fearfull to name)

HAVE BROAK FORTH OFTENER THAN ONCE
IN THIS LAND

2

indicted for ye same) with
a mare, a cowe, tow goats, five sheep, 2. calves
and a turkey   (Plymouth Plantation)

Now follows ye ministers answers

3

Mr Charles Channcys   a reverend, godly, very larned man
who shortly thereafter, due to a difference aboute baptising
he holding it ought only to be by diping
that sprinkling was unlawful, removed him selfe
to the same Sityate, a minister to ye church ther

in this case proved, by reference to ye judicials of Moyses
& see: Luther, Calvin, Hen: Bulin:. Theo: Beza. Zanch:
what greevous sin in ye sight of God,
by ye instigation of burning lusts, set on fire of hell,
to proceede to contactum & fricationem ad emissionem seminis,
    &c.,
& y^t contra naturam, or to attempt ye grosse acts of

4

Mr Bradford: I forbear perticulers.
And accordingly he was cast by ye jury,
and condemned.

It being demanded of him
the youth confessed he had it of another
who had long used it in old England,
and they kept catle togeather.

And after executed about ye 8. of Sept^r, 1642.
A very sade spectakle it was; for first the mare,
and then ye cowe, and ye rest of ye lesser catle,
were kild before his face, according to ye law
Levit: 20.15.

and then he him selfe

                              and no use made of any part of them

JOSEPHINE MILES

Miss Miles (born 1911, Chicago, Illinois, attended the University of California, Los Angeles, and the University of California, Berkeley) has taught for many years at the University of California, Berkeley. The poems are from *Prefabrications* (1955), and *Kinds of Affection* (1967).

RIDE

It's not my world, I grant, but I made it.
It's not my ranch, lean oak, buzzard crow,
Not my fryers, mixmaster, well-garden.
And now it's down the road and I made it.

It's not your rackety car but you drive it.
It's not your four-door, top-speed, white-wall tires,
Not our state, not even, I guess, our nation,
But now it's down the road, and we're in it.

AUTUMNAL

We have lost so many leaves
   in loss, loss, loss
Out of the sky,
What shall we do for shelter to live by?

Not roof shelter, but leaf shelter,
   the tentative
Crosswise cover
Which a thousand light ideas give.

Retire under somebody's constructed rafters
   or be grieved that a truthful brain
Exists under a truthful sky
With no palaver between.

YESTERDAY EVENING AS THE SUN SET LATE

Yesterday evening as the sun set late,
    We parked at Land's End, past the Golden Gate,
    To see the cypress lean in from that ocean,
    And the wave-path lengthen to the lengthening sun.
    In the VW over beside us, a yellow-haired girl
    Looked at us with a radiance
    Hardly receivable. We smiled and turned
    Back to the sea as she held out her arms to us.
    Her blown voice said to the three with her,
    I know why you brought me here,
    To love these mixed-up people, and I do!
    See, they are smiling at me, poor sad
    Mixed-up people! Her friends sheltering
    Walked with her to the cliff's edge.
    Deep to the rocks, far to the falling sun,
    She reached her hand. She saw her hand,
    Held it close to her eyes, widened its fingers,
    Hand translucent. Who will keep it? She put it
    Inside the coat of the yellow-haired boy and he leaned
    Over her like the wind.
    When she came back to the car she had lost her hand,
    Lost us. We said goodbye as they drove off.
    A trawler crossed between us and the sun.

THIS LAND IS YOUR LAND*

This land is your land,
This land is my land,
From California to the New York island,
From the redwood forest to the Gulf Stream waters,
This land was made for you and me.

As I was walking that ribbon of highway,
I saw above me that endless skyway,
I saw below me that golden valley,
This land was made for you and me.

This land is your land,
This land is my land,
From California to the New York island,
From the redwood forest to the Gulf Stream waters,
This land was made for you and me.

I've roamed and rambled and I followed my footsteps,
To the sparkling sands of her diamond deserts,
And all around me a voice was sounding,
This land was made for you and me.

This land is your land,
This land is my land,
From California to the New York island,
From the redwood forest to the Gulf Stream waters,
This land was made for you and me.

When the sun comes shining as I was strolling,
And the wheatfields waving and the dust clouds rolling,
As the fog was lifting, a voice was chanting,
This land was made for you and me.

—Woody Guthrie

*TRO— ©copyright 1956 and 1958 Ludlow Music Inc., New York, N.Y. Used with permission of Publisher. All rights reserved.

WOODY GUTHRIE

By the age of thirteen Woody Guthrie (born 1912, Okemah, Oklahoma) was on his own. He made his living by odd jobs like sign painting, and rode a freight to California during the Depression, and came to share a fifteen-minute radio program with his cousin in Los Angeles. Between 1932 and 1952 he wrote more than 1000 songs. In 1955 he began to grow ill from a progressive disease of the nervous system. In 1967 he died. The songs are taken from *The Very Best of Popular Folk Music* (Hollis Music).

PASTURES OF PLENTY*

It's a mighty hard row that my poor hands have hoed,
My poor feet have traveled a hot dusty road,
Out of your dustbowl and westward we roll,
And your desert was hot and your mountains was cold.

I've worked in your orchards of peaches and prunes,
Slept on the ground in the light of your moon,
On the edge of your city you've seen us and then
We come with the dust and we go with the wind.

California and Arizona, I make all your crops,
And it's north up to Oregon to gather your hops,
Dig the beets from your ground, cut grapes from your vines,
To set on your tables your light sparkling wine.

Green pastures of plenty from dry desert ground,
From that Grand Coulee dam where the water runs down,
Every state in this Union us migrants have been,
We work in your fight, and we'll fight til we win.

Well, it's always we ramble, that river and I,
All along your green valley I'll work til I die,
My land I'll defend with my life, if it be,
'Cause my pastures of plenty must always be free.

*TRO— © copyright 1960 and 1963 Ludlow Music Inc., New York, N.Y. Used with permission of Publisher. All rights reserved.

PLANE WRECK AT LOS GATOS*
(DEPORTEE) (GOODBYE, JUAN)

The crops are all in and the peaches are rott'ning,
The oranges piled in their creosote dumps.
You're flying 'em back to the Mexican border,
To pay all their money to wade back again.

Goodbye to my Juan, goodbye, Rosalita,
Adios mis amigos, Jesus y Maria.
You won't have your names when you ride the big airplane,
All they will call you will be deportees.

My father's own father, he waded that river,
They took all the money he made in his life.
My brothers and sisters come working the fruit trees,
And they rode the truck till they took down and died.

Goodbye to my Juan, goodbye, Rosalita,
Adios mis amigos, Jesus y Maria.
You won't have your names when you ride the big airplane,
All they will call you will be deportees.

Some of us are illegal, and some are not wanted,
Our work contract's out and we have to move on.
Six hundred miles to that Mexican border,
They chase us like outlaws, like rustlers, like thieves.

Goodbye to my Juan, goodbye, Rosalita,
Adios mis amigos, Jesus y Maria.
You won't have your names when you ride the big airplane,
All they will call you will be deportees.

We died in your hills, we died in your deserts,
We died in your valleys and died on your plains.
We died 'neath your trees and we died in your bushes,
Both sides of the river, we died just the same.

*TRO— © copyright 1961 and 1963 Ludlow Music Inc., New York, N.Y. Used with permission of Publisher. All rights reserved.

WOODY GUTHRIE

Goodbye to my Juan, goodbye, Rosalita,
Adios mis amigos, Jesus y Maria.
You won't have your names when you ride the big airplane,
All they will call you will be deportees.

The sky plane caught fire over Los Gatos Canyon,
A fireball of lightning, and shook all our hills.
Who are all these friends, all scattered like dry leaves?
The radio says they are just deportees.

Goodbye to my Juan, goodbye, Rosalita,
Adios mis amigos, Jesus y Maria.
You won't have your names when you ride the big airplane,
All they will call you will be deportees.

Is this the best way we can grow our big orchards?
Is this the best way we can grow our good fruit?
To fall like dry leaves to rot on my topsoil
And be called by no name except deportees?

Goodbye to my Juan, goodbye, Rosalita,
Adios mis amigos, Jesus y Maria.
You won't have your names when you ride the big airplane,
All they will call you will be deportees.

MAIL MYSELF TO YOU*

I'm gonna wrap myself in paper,
I'm gonna daub myself with glue,
Stick some stamps on top of my head,
I'm gonna mail myself to you.

I'm agonna tie me up in a red string,
I'm gonna tie blue ribbons too,
I'm agonna climb up in my mail box,
I'm gonna mail myself to you.

*TRO— ©copyright 1962 and 1963 Ludlow Music Inc., New York, N.Y. Used with permission of Publisher. All rights reserved.

When you see me in your mail box,
Cut the string and let me out,
Wash the glue off my fingers,
Stick some bubblegum in my mouth.

Take me out of my wrapping paper,
Wash the stamps off my head,
Pour me full of ice cream sodies,
Put me in my nice warm bed.

I'm gonna wrap myself in paper,
I'm gonna daub myself with glue,
Stick some stamps on top of my head,
I'm gonna mail myself to you.

ROBERT HAYDEN

Robert Hayden was born in 1913 in Detroit, Michigan. He attended Wayne State University and the University of Michigan, and is now Professor of English at Fisk University. In 1965, he was awarded the Grand Prize for Poetry at the First World Festival of Negro Arts in Dakar, Senegal, for his book of poetry *A Ballad for Remembrance*. He is poetry editor of *World Order,* the Baha'i magazine.

"Middle Passage" is from *Selected Poems* (1966). In a note Hayden states that Part Three of the poem "follows, in the main, the account of the *Amistad* mutiny given by Muriel Rukeyser [a poet] in her biography of Willard Gibbs."

MIDDLE PASSAGE

I.

Jesús, Estrella, Esperanza, Mercy:

    Sails flashing to the wind like weapons,
    sharks following the moans the fever and the dying;
    horror the corposant and compass rose.

Middle Passage:
        voyage through death
                to life upon these shores.

    "10 April 1800—
    Blacks rebellious. Crew uneasy. Our linguist says
    their moaning is a prayer for death,
    ours and their own. Some try to starve themselves.
    Lost three this morning leaped with crazy laughter
    to the waiting sharks, sang as they went under."

Desire, Adventure, Tartar, Ann:

    Standing to America, bringing home
    black gold, black ivory, black seed.

> *Deep in the festering hold thy father lies,*
> *of his bones New England pews are made,*
> *those are altar lights that were his eyes.*

Jesus Saviour Pilot Me
Over Life's Tempestuous Sea

We pray that Thou wilt grant, O Lord,
safe passage to our vessels bringing
heathen souls unto Thy chastening.

Jesus Saviour

> "8 bells. I cannot sleep, for I am sick
> with fear, but writing eases fear a little
> since still my eyes can see these words take shape
> upon the page & so I write, as one
> would turn to exorcism. 4 days scudding,
> but now the sea is calm again. Misfortune
> follows in our wake like sharks (our grinning
> tutelary gods). Which one of us
> has killed an albatross? A plague among
> our blacks—Ophthalmia: blindness—& we
> have jettisoned the blind to no avail.
> It spreads, the terrifying sickness spreads.
> Its claws have scratched sight from the Capt.'s eyes
> & there is blindness in the fo'c'sle
> & we must sail 3 weeks before we come to port."

> *What port awaits us, Davy Jones'*
> *or home? I've heard of slavers drifting, drifting,*
> *playthings of wind and storm and chance, their crews*
> *gone blind, the jungle hatred*
> *crawling up on deck.*

Thou Who Walked On Galilee

> "Deponent further sayeth *The Bella J*
> left the Guinea Coast
> with cargo of five hundred blacks and odd
> for the barracoons of Florida:

"That there was hardly room 'tween-decks for half
the sweltering cattle stowed spoon-fashion there;
that some went mad of thirst and tore their flesh
and sucked the blood:

"That Crew and Captain lusted with the comeliest
of the savage girls kept naked in the cabins;
that there was one they called The Guinea Rose
and they cast lots and fought to lie with her:

"That when the Bo's'n piped all hands, the flames
spreading from starboard already were beyond
control, the negroes howling and their chains
entangled with the flames:

"That the burning blacks could not be reached,
that the Crew abandoned ship,
leaving their shrieking negresses behind,
that the Captain perished drunken with the wenches:

"Further Deponent sayeth not."

Pilot Oh Pilot Me

II.

Aye, lad, and I have seen those factories,
Gambia, Rio Pongo, Calabar;
have watched the artful mongos baiting traps
of war wherein the victor and the vanquished

Were caught as prizes for our barracoons.
Have seen the nigger kings whose vanity
and greed turned wild black hides of Fellatah,
Mandingo, Ibo, Kru to gold for us.

And there was one—King Anthracite we named him—
fetish face beneath French parasols
of brass and orange velvet, impudent mouth
whose cups were carven skulls of enemies:

He'd honor us with drum and feast and conjo
and palm-oil-glistening wenches deft in love,
and for tin crowns that shone with paste,
red calico and German-silver trinkets

Would have the drums talk war and send
his warriors to burn the sleeping villages
and kill the sick and old and lead the young
in coffles to our factories.

Twenty years a trader, twenty years,
for there was wealth aplenty to be harvested
from those black fields, and I'd be trading still
but for the fevers melting down my bones.

III.

Shuttles in the rocking loom of history,
the dark ships move, the dark ships move,
their bright ironical names
like jests of kindness on a murderer's mouth;
plough through thrashing glister toward
fata morgana's lucent melting shore,
weave toward New World littorals that are
mirage and myth and actual shore.

Voyage through death,
voyage whose chartings are unlove.

A charnel stench, effluvium of living death
spreads outward from the hold,
where the living and the dead, the horribly dying,
lie interlocked, lie foul with blood and excrement.

>   *Deep in the festering hold thy father lies,*
>   *the corpse of mercy rots with him,*
>   *rats eat love's rotten gelid eyes.*
>
>   *But, oh, the living look at you*
>   *with human eyes whose suffering accuses you,*
>   *whose hatred reaches through the swill of dark*
>   *to strike you like a leper's claw.*
>
>   *You cannot stare that hatred down*
>   *or chain the fear that stalks the watches*
>   *and breathes on you its fetid scorching breath;*
>   *cannot kill the deep immortal human wish,*
>   *the timeless will.*

"But for the storm that flung up barriers
of wind and wave, *The Amistad,* señores,
would have reached the port of Príncipe in two,
three days at most; but for the storm we should
have been prepared for what befell.
Swift as the puma's leap it came. There was
that interval of moonless calm filled only
with the water's and the rigging's usual sounds,
then sudden movement, blows and snarling cries
and they had fallen on us with machete
and marlinspike. It was as though the very
air, the night itself were stroking us.
Exhausted by the rigors of the storm,
we were no match for them. Our men went down
before the murderous Africans. Our loyal
Celestino ran from below with gun
and lantern and I saw, before the cane-
knife's wounding flash, Cinquez,
that surly brute who calls himself a prince,
directing, urging on the ghastly work.
He hacked the poor mulatto down, and then
he turned on me. The decks were slippery
when daylight finally came. It sickens me
to think of what I saw, of how these apes
threw overboard the butchered bodies of
our men, true Christians all, like so much jetsam.
Enough, enough. The rest is quickly told:
Cinquez was forced to spare the two of us
you see to steer the ship to Africa,
and we like phantoms doomed to rove the sea
voyaged east by day and west by night,
deceiving them, hoping for rescue,
prisoners on our own vessel, till
at length we drifted to the shores of this
your land, America, where we were freed
from our unspeakable misery. Now we
demand, good sirs, the extradition of
Cinquez and his accomplices to La
Havana. And it distresses us to know
there are so many here who seem inclined
to justify the mutiny of these blacks.

> We find it paradoxical indeed
> that you whose wealth, whose tree of liberty
> are rooted in the labor of your slaves
> should suffer the august John Quincy Adams
> to speak with so much passion of the right
> of chattel slaves to kill their lawful masters
> and with his Roman rhetoric weave a hero's
> garland for Cinquez. I tell you that
> we are determined to return to Cuba
> with our slaves and there see justice done. Cinquez—
> or let us say 'the Prince'—Cinquez shall die."

The deep immortal human wish,
the timeless will:

> Cinquez its deathless primaveral image,
> life that transfigures many lives.

Voyage through death
                  to life upon these shores.

WELDON KEES

Weldon Kees was a man of many talents. He was born in 1914 in Beatrice, Nebraska, and attended the University of Nebraska. During the thirties he wrote fiction for literary magazines in the midwest and worked as an editor on a federal writer's project. Later he was director of the Bibliographical Center of Research for the Rocky Mountain region. He left the Midwest for New York City, worked there as a writer for *Time* magazine, and became a painter and a maker of documentary films. During the fifties he lived on the West Coast, studied the piano, and composed in the jazz manner. He also worked as a professional photographer. In 1955 he left his car near the Golden Gate Bridge and disappeared. The poems are from *The Collected Poems* (1960), edited by Donald Justice, whose introduction includes the information given above.

FOR MY DAUGHTER

Looking into my daughter's eyes I read
Beneath the innocence of morning flesh
Concealed, hintings of death she does not heed.
Coldest of winds have blown this hair, and mesh
Of seaweed snarled these miniatures of hands;
The night's slow poison, tolerant and bland,
Has moved her blood. Parched years that I have seen
That may be hers appear: foul, lingering
Death in certain war, the slim legs green.
Or, fed on hate, she relishes the sting
Of others' agony; perhaps the cruel
Bride of a syphilitic or a fool.
These speculations sour in the sun.
I have no daughter. I desire none.

WHITE COLLAR BALLAD

There are lots of places to go:
Guaranteed headaches at every club,
Plush-and-golden cinemas that always show
How cunningly the heroine and hero rub.
Put on your hat, put on your gloves.
But there isn't any love, there isn't any love.

There are endless things we could do:
Walk around the block, watch the skaters whirl,
Promenade the park or see the newest zoo,
Plan for the future in a sensible world.
The water boils on the stove,
But there isn't any love, there isn't any love.

Our best friends lived in the house next door.
Went around to call on them the other day,
But they hadn't left an address or a word before
They packed their bags and moved away.
We could call on the people on the floor above,
But there wouldn't be any love, there wouldn't be any love.

It didn't use to be like this at all.
You wanted lots of money and I got it somehow.
Once it was Summer. Here it's almost Fall.
It isn't any season now.
There are seasons in the future to be thinking of,
But there won't be any love, there won't be any love.

ROBINSON

The dog stops barking after Robinson has gone.
His act is over. The world is a gray world,
Not without violence, and he kicks under the grand piano,
The nightmare chase well under way.

The mirror from Mexico, stuck to the wall,
Reflects nothing at all. The glass is black.
Robinson alone provides the image Robinsonian.

Which is all of the room—walls, curtains,
Shelves, bed, the tinted photograph of Robinson's first wife,
Rugs, vases, panatellas in a humidor.
They would fill the room if Robinson came in.

The pages in the books are blank,
The books that Robinson has read. That is his favorite chair,
Or where the chair would be if Robinson were here.

All day the phone rings. It could be Robinson
Calling. It never rings when he is here.

Outside, white buildings yellow in the sun.
Outside, the birds circle continuously
Where trees are actual and take no holiday.

WILLIAM STAFFORD

William Stafford (born 1914, Hutchinson, Kansas; attended the University of Kansas and the University of Iowa) teaches in the English department of Lewis and Clark College, near Portland, Oregon. The poem comes from *Traveling Through the Dark* (1962).

TRAVELING THROUGH THE DARK

Traveling through the dark I found a deer
dead on the edge of the Wilson River road.
It is usually best to roll them into the canyon:
that road is narrow; to swerve might make more dead.

By glow of the tail-light I stumbled back of the car
and stood by the heap, a doe, a recent killing;
she had stiffened already, almost cold.
I dragged her off; she was large in the belly.

My fingers touching her side brought me the reason—
her side was warm; her fawn lay there waiting,
alive, still, never to be born.
Beside that mountain road I hesitated.

The car aimed ahead its lowered parking lights;
under the hood purred the steady engine.
I stood in the glare of the warm exhaust turning red;
around our group I could hear the wilderness listen.

I thought hard for us all—my only swerving—,
then pushed her over the edge into the river.

RANDALL JARRELL

Randall Jarrell was born in 1914 in Nashville, Tennessee. He attended Vanderbilt and Princeton, and he died in 1965 in Greensboro, North Carolina. During World War II he served in the Air Corps as a flyer and instructor. He later taught English at several colleges and universities, among them Kenyon College, where he and Robert Lowell became friends. His post of longest tenure was a professorship at the Women's College of the University of North Carolina, Greensboro. He was literary editor of *The Nation* magazine, and he served a term as poetry consultant at the Library of Congress in Washington, D.C. He is the author of a very funny academic novel, *Pictures from an Institution* (1954), and of several collections of essays. The poems are from *The Complete Poems* (1969).

COME TO THE STONE . . .

The child saw the bombers skate like stones across the fields
As he trudged down the ways the summer strewed
With its reluctant foliage; how many giants
Rose and peered down and vanished, by the road
The ants had littered with their crumbs and dead.

"That man is white and red like my clown doll,"
He says to his mother, who has gone away.
"I didn't cry, I didn't cry."
In the sky the planes are angry like the wind.
The people are punishing the people—why?

He answers easily, his foolish eyes
Brightening at that long simile, the world.
The angels sway above his story like balloons.
A child makes everything—except his death—a child's.
Come to the stone and tell me why I died.

THE DEATH OF THE BALL TURRET GUNNER

From my mother's sleep I fell into the State,
And I hunched in its belly till my wet fur froze.
Six miles from earth, loosed from its dream of life,
I woke to black flak and the nightmare fighters.
When I died they washed me out of the turret with a hose.

THE SICK NOUGHT

Do the wife and baby travelling to see
Your grey pajamas and sick worried face
Remind you of something, soldier? I remember
You convalescing washing plates, or mopping
The endless corridors your shoes had scuffed;
And in the crowded room you rubbed your cheek
Against your wife's thin elbow like a pony.
But you are something there are millions of.
How can I care about you much, or pick you out
From all the others other people loved
And sent away to die for them? You are a ticket
Someone bought and lost on, a stray animal:
You have lost even the right to be condemned.
I see you looking helplessly around, in histories,
Bewildered with your terrible companions, Pain
And Death and Empire: what have you understood, to die?
Were you worth, soldiers, all that people said
To be spent so willingly? Surely your one theory, to live,
Is nonsense to the practice of the centuries.
What is demanded in the trade of states
But lives, your lives?—the one commodity.

GWENDOLYN BROOKS

Gwendolyn Brooks (born 1917, Topeka, Kansas) grew up in Chicago, attended Wilson Junior College (Chicago), and succeeded Carl Sandburg as Poet Laureate of Illinois. She has taught in various schools and colleges, most recently Northeastern Illinois State College, Columbia College (Chicago), and Elmhurst College (Elmhurst, Illinois). In 1950 she won the Pulitzer Prize for poetry. She is married, with two children, and lives in Chicago. The poems come from *Selected Poems* (1963).

SADIE AND MAUD

Maud went to college.
Sadie stayed at home.
Sadie scraped life
With a fine-tooth comb.

She didn't leave a tangle in.
Her comb found every strand.
Sadie was one of the livingest chits
In all the land.

Sadie bore two babies
Under her maiden name.
Maud and Ma and Papa
Nearly died of shame.

When Sadie said her last so-long
Her girls struck out from home.
(Sadie had left as heritage
Her fine-tooth comb.)

Maud, who went to college,
Is a thin brown mouse.
She is living all alone
In this old house.

JESSIE MITCHELL'S MOTHER

Into her mother's bedroom to wash the ballooning body.
"My mother is jelly-hearted and she has a brain of jelly:
Sweet, quiver-soft, irrelevant. Not essential.
Only a habit would cry if she should die.
A pleasant sort of fool without the least iron. . . .
Are you better, mother, do you think it will come today?"
The stretched yellow rag that was Jessie Mitchell's mother
Reviewed her. Young, and so thin, and so straight.
So straight! as if nothing could ever bend her.
But poor men would bend her, and doing things with poor men,
Being much in bed, and babies would bend her over,
And the rest of things in life that were for poor women,
Coming to them grinning and pretty with intent to bend and to kill.
Comparisons shattered her heart, ate at her bulwarks:
The shabby and the bright: she, almost hating her daughter,
Crept into an old sly refuge: "Jessie's black
And her way will be black, and jerkier even than mine.
Mine, in fact, because I was lovely, had flowers
Tucked in the jerks, flowers were here and there. . . ."
She revived for the moment settled and dried-up triumphs,
Forced perfume into old petals, pulled up the droop,
Refueled
Triumphant long-exhaled breaths.
Her exquisite yellow youth . . .

WE REAL COOL

The Pool Players.
Seven at the Golden Shovel.

We real cool. We
Left school. We

Lurk late. We
Strike straight. We

Sing sin. We
Thin gin. We

Jazz June. We
Die soon.

from THE WOMANHOOD (Section VIII)

Beverly Hills, Chicago

"and the people live till they have white hair"
       —E. M. Price

The dry brown coughing beneath their feet,
(Only a while, for the handyman is on his way)
These people walk their golden gardens.
We say ourselves fortunate to be driving by today.

That we may look at them, in their gardens where
The summer ripeness rots. But not raggedly.
Even the leaves fall down in lovelier patterns here.
And the refuse, the refuse is a neat brilliancy.

When they flow sweetly into their houses
With softness and slowness touched by that everlasting gold,
We know what they go to. To tea. But that does not mean
They will throw some little black dots into some water and add sugar
  and the juice of the cheapest lemons that are sold,

While downstairs that woman's vague phonograph bleats,
  "Knock me a kiss."
And the living all to be made again in the sweatingest physical manner
Tomorrow. . . . Not that anybody is saying that these people have no
  trouble.
Merely that it is trouble with a gold-flecked beautiful banner.

Nobody is saying that these people do not ultimately cease to be. And
Sometimes their passings are even more painful than ours.
It is just that so often they live till their hair is white.
They make excellent corpses, among the expensive flowers. . . .

Nobody is furious. Nobody hates these people.
At least, nobody driving by in this car.
It is only natural, however, that it should occur to us
How much more fortunate they are than we are.

It is only natural that we should look and look
At their wood and brick and stone
And think, while a breath of pine blows,
How different these are from our own.

We do not want them to have less.
But it is only natural that we should think we have not enough.
We drive on, we drive on.
When we speak to each other our voices are a little gruff.

ROBERT LOWELL

Lowell is an old name in New England, as is Winslow, the family name of Robert Lowell's mother. Robert Lowell was born in 1917 in Boston, Massachusetts, attended Harvard, Kenyon College, and Louisiana State University, and has taught in the English departments of several colleges and universities, among them Boston University, where Anne Sexton and Sylvia Plath attended his seminar in poetry writing. He has written plays based upon works by Nathaniel Hawthorne and Herman Melville and has made translations, which he calls "imitations," of poems and plays from classical and modern languages. He lives in New York City with his wife Elizabeth Hardwick, a writer. The poems are taken from *Lord Weary's Castle* (1946), *Life Studies* (1959), and *For the Union Dead* (1964).

CHILDREN OF LIGHT

Our fathers wrung their bread from stocks and stones
And fenced their gardens with the Redman's bones;
Embarking from the Nether Land of Holland,
Pilgrims unhouseled by Geneva's night,
They planted here the Serpent's seeds of light;
And here the pivoting searchlights probe to shock
The riotous glass houses built on rock,
And candles gutter by an empty altar,
And light is where the landless blood of Cain
Is burning, burning the unburied grain.

MEMORIES OF WEST STREET AND LEPKE

Only teaching on Tuesdays, book-worming
in pajamas fresh from the washer each morning,
I hog a whole house on Boston's
"hardly passionate Marlborough Street,"
where even the man
scavenging filth in the back alley trash cans,
has two children, a beach wagon, a helpmate,
and is a "young Republican."
I have a nine months' daughter,
young enough to be my granddaughter.
Like the sun she rises in her flame-flamingo infants' wear.

These are the tranquillized *Fifties,*
and I am forty. Ought I to regret my seedtime?
I was a fire-breathing Catholic C. O.,
and made my manic statement,
telling off the state and president, and then
sat waiting sentence in the bull pen
beside a Negro boy with curlicues
of marijuana in his hair.

Given a year,
I walked on the roof of the West Street Jail, a short
enclosure like my school soccer court,
and saw the Hudson River once a day
through sooty clothesline entanglements
and bleaching khaki tenements.
Strolling, I yammered metaphysics with Abramowitz,
a jaundice-yellow ("it's really tan")
and fly-weight pacifist,
so vegetarian,
he wore rope shoes and preferred fallen fruit.
He tried to convert Bioff and Brown,
the Hollywood pimps, to his diet.
Hairy, muscular, suburban,
wearing chocolate double-breasted suits,
they blew their tops and beat him black and blue.

I was so out of things, I'd never heard
of the Jehovah's Witnesses.
"Are you a C. O.?" I asked a fellow jailbird.
"No," he answered, "I'm a J.W."
He taught me the "hospital tuck,"
and pointed out the T shirted back
of *Murder Incorporated's* Czar Lepke,
there piling towels on a rack,
or dawdling off to his little segregated cell full
of things forbidden the common man:
a portable radio, a dresser, two toy American
flags tied together with a ribbon of Easter palm.
Flabby, bald, lobotomized,
he drifted in a sheepish calm,
where no agonizing reappraisal
jarred his concentration on the electric chair—
hanging like an oasis in his air
of lost connections. . . .

THE MOUTH OF THE HUDSON

A single man stands like a bird-watcher,
and scuffles the pepper and salt snow
from a discarded, gray
Westinghouse Electric cable drum.
He cannot discover America by counting
the chains of condemned
freight-trains
from thirty states. They jolt and jar
and junk in the siding below him.
He has trouble with his balance.
His eyes drop,
and he drifts with the wild ice
ticking seaward down the Hudson,
like the blank sides of a jig-saw puzzle.

The ice ticks seaward like a clock.
A Negro toasts
wheat-seeds over the coke-fumes
of a punctured barrel.
Chemical air
sweeps in from New Jersey,
and smells of coffee.

Across the river
ledges of suburban factories tan
in the sulphur-yellow sun
of the unforgivable landscape.

FOR THE UNION DEAD

"Relinquunt Omnia Servare Rem Publicam."[1]

The old South Boston Aquarium stands
in a Sahara of snow now. Its broken windows are boarded.
The bronze weathervane cod has lost half its scales.
The airy tanks are dry.

Once my nose crawled like a snail on the glass;
my hand tingled
to burst the bubbles
drifting from the noses of the cowed, compliant fish.

My hand draws back. I often sigh still
for the dark downward and vegetating kingdom
of the fish and reptile. One morning last March,
I pressed against the new barbed and galvanized

fence on the Boston Common. Behind their cage,
yellow dinosaur steamshovels were grunting
as they cropped up tons of mush and grass
to gouge their underworld garage.

Parking spaces luxuriate like civic
sandpiles in the heart of Boston.
A girdle of orange, Puritan-pumpkin colored girders
braces the tingling Statehouse,

shaking over the excavations, as it faces Colonel Shaw
and his bell-cheeked Negro infantry
on St. Gaudens' shaking Civil War relief,[2]
propped by a plank splint against the garage's earthquake.

Two months after marching through Boston,
half the regiment was dead;
at the dedication,
William James could almost hear the bronze Negroes breathe.[3]

Their monument sticks like a fishbone
in the city's throat.
Its Colonel is as lean
as a compass-needle.

He has an angry wrenlike vigilance,
a greyhound's gentle tautness;
he seems to wince at pleasure,
and suffocate for privacy.

He is out of bounds now. He rejoices in man's lovely,
peculiar power to choose life and die—
when he leads his black soldiers to death,
he cannot bend his back.

On a thousand small town New England greens,
the old white churches hold their air
of sparse, sincere rebellion; frayed flags
quilt the graveyards of the Grand Army of the Republic.

The stone statues of the abstract Union Soldier
grow slimmer and younger each year—
wasp-wasted, they doze over muskets
and muse through their sideburns . . .

Shaw's father wanted no monument
except the ditch,
where his son's body was thrown
and lost with his "niggers."

The ditch is nearer.
There are no statues for the last war here;
on Boyleston Street, a commercial photograph
shows Hiroshima boiling

over a Mosler Safe, the "Rock of Ages"
that survived the blast. Space is nearer.
When I crouch to my television set,
the drained faces of Negro school-children rise like balloons.

Colonel Shaw
is riding on his bubble,
he waits
for the blesséd break.

The Aquarium is gone. Everywhere,
giant finned cars nose forward like fish;
a savage servility
slides by on grease.

   ¹*"Relinquunt Omnia Servare Rem Publicam"* "They give up everything to save the republic." ²*St. Gaudens* (1848-1907) was a sculptor. A relief is a sculpture in which rounded figures project from a flat background. ³*William James* (1842-1910) was a teacher at Harvard, philosopher, psychologist, and the brother of Henry James, the novelist.

LAWRENCE FERLINGHETTI

Born 1919, Yonkers, New York, or Paris, France; attended the University of North Carolina, Columbia and the Sorbonne (Paris). Since 1953 Lawrence Ferlinghetti has owned the City Lights Bookstore in San Francisco and has headed a publishing house called City Lights. In 1956 he brought out *Howl and Other Poems* by Allen Ginsberg. Other poets in his *Pocket Poets* series are Gregory Corso, Denise Levertov, Bob Kaufman, Robert Bly, and Frank O'Hara. The poems are taken from *A Coney Island of the Mind* (1958) and *The Secret Meaning of Things* (1969).

IN GOYA'S GREATEST SCENES WE SEEM TO SEE

In Goya's greatest scenes we seem to see
                                        the people of the world
            exactly at the moment when
                    they first attained the title of
                                    'suffering humanity'
            They writhe upon the page
                        in a veritable rage
                                    of adversity
        Heaped up
                groaning with babies and bayonets
                                        under cement skies
            in an abstract landscape of blasted trees
            bent statues bats wings and beaks
                    slippery gibbets
            cadavers and carnivorous cocks
            and all the final hollering monsters
                of the
                        'imagination of disaster'
            they are so bloody real
                        it is as if they really still existed

    And they do

            Only the landscape is changed

    They still are ranged along the roads
        plagued by legionaires
                false windmills and demented roosters

They are the same people
                only further from home
    on freeways fifty lanes wide
        on a concrete continent
            spaced with bland billboards
      illustrating imbecile illusions of happiness

The scene shows fewer tumbrils
            but more maimed citizens
                in painted cars
  and they have strange license plates
and engines
        that devour America

AFTER THE CRIES OF THE BIRDS

Hurrying thru eternity
        after the cries of the birds has stopped
I see the "future of the world"
        in a new visionary society
        now only dimly recognizable
        in folk-rock ballrooms
        free-form dancers in ecstatic clothing
            their hearts their gurus
            every man his own myth
            butterflies in amber
                    caught fucking life
    hurrying thru eternity
                to a new pastoral era
I see the shadows of that future
      in that white island
               which is San Francisco
      floating in its foreign sea
                seen high on a hill
                in the Berkeley Rose Garden
      looking West at sunset to the Golden Gate
        adrift in its Japanese landscape

                    under Mt. Tamal-Fuji[1]
                    with its grazing bulls
                                        hurrying thru heaven
            the city with its white buildings
                        "a temple to some unknown god"
                            (as Voznesensky[2] said)
        after the cries of the birds has stopped
            I see the sea come in
                            over South San Francisco
        and the island of the city
                            truly floated free at last
        never really a part of America
            East East and West West
                    and the twain met long ago
    in "the wish to pursue what lies beyond the mind"
        and with no place to go but In
                        after Columbus recovered America
    and the West Coast captured by some Spanish Catholics
        cagily getting the jump by sea
            coveredwagons crawling over lost plains
                                hung up in Oklahoma
                Prairie schooners into Pullmans
    while whole tribes of Indians
                        shake hopeless feather lances
            and disappear over the horizon
    to reappear centuries later
                        feet up and smoking wild cigars
            at the corner of Hollywood & Vine
    hurrying thru eternity
                must we wait for the cries of the birds
                                        to be stopped

                        before we dig In
    after centuries of running
                up & down the Coast of West
        looking for the right place to jump off
                                further Westward
        the Gutenberg Galaxy[3] casts its light no further
            the "Westward march of civilization"

   comes to a dead stop on the shores of
    Big Sur Portland & Santa Monica
    and turns upon itself at last
     after the cries of the birds has stopped
must we wait for that
       to dig a new model
      of the universe
       with instant communication
      a world village
     in which every human being is a part of us
   though we be still throw-aways
       in an evolutionary progression
as Spengler[4] reverses himself
    Mark Twain meets Jack London
     and turns back to Mississippi
      shaking his head
  and the Last Frontier
      having no place to go but In
  can't face it
    and buries its head
Western civilization gone too far West
       might suffer a sea-change
   into Something Else Eastern
       and that won't do

the Chinese are coming anyway
        time we prepared their tea
  Gunga Din[5] still with us
    Kipling[6] nods & cries *I told you so!*
    the French King hollers *Merde!*[7]
    and abandons his Vietnam bordel
but not us
    we love them too much for that
  though the Mayflower turned around sets sail again
   back to Plymouth England (and the Piltdown letdown)
   misjudging the coast & landing in Loverpool
   American poets capture Royal Albert Hall
    The Jefferson Airplane takes off
        and circles heaven

LAWRENCE FERLINGHETTI

              It all figures
                          in a new litany
                                          probably pastoral
          after the cries of the birds has stopped
                Rose petals fall
                              in the Berkeley Rose Garden
        where I sit trying to remember
                              the lines about rose leaves
            in the *Four Quartets*[8]
                              Stella kisses her lover in the sunset
                                          under an arbor
                    A Los Angeles actor nearby goes *Zap! Zap!*
                                          at the setting sun
        It is the end
                          I drop downhill
                into a reception for Anais Nin[9]
                              with a paperbag full of rose leaves

            She is autographing her Book
                  I empty the bag over her head from behind
                  Her gold lacquered hair sheds the petals
                        They tumble red & yellow on her signed book
                  Girl again she presses them between the leaves
                              delightedly
                                          like fallen friends
                    Her words
                                  flame in my heart
            Virginia Woolf[10] under water
                                      she drifts away on the book
              a leaf herself blowing skittered
                                              over the horizon
            The wish to pursue what lies beyond the mind
                              lies just beyond
                  Ask a flower what it does
                              to move beyond the senses
              Our cells hate metal
                              The tide turns
                  We shoot holes in the clouds' trousers
                        and napalm sears the hillsides
                    skips a bridge

            narrows to a grass hut full of charred bodies
         and is later reported looking like
                    "The eternal flame at Kennedy's grave"
            A tree flowers red It can't run
Shall we now advance into the 21st century?
         I see the lyric future of the world
            on the beaches of Big Sur[11]
                gurus at Jack's Flats
            nude swart maidens swimming
               in pools of sunlight
                Kali[12] on the beach
            guitarists with one earring
         lovely birds in long dresses and Indian headbands

                    What does this have to do with Lenin?
            Plenty!
   Die-hard Maoists lie down together crosswise
                        and out comes a string
                            of Chinese firecrackers
               and after the cries of the birds
                            has stopped
            Chinese junks show up suddenly
                off the coast of Big Sur
            filled with more than Chinese philosophers
                        dreaming they are butterflies
How shall we greet them? Are we ready
                        to receive them?
            Shall we put out koan[13] steppingstones
                            scrolls & bowls
         greet them with agape
            Tu Fu and bamboo flutes at midnight?
            Big Sur junk meet
                Chinese junk?
Will they ride the breakers into Bixby cove?
   Will they bring their women with them
         Will we take them on the beach
   like Ron Boise's lovers[14] in Kama Sutra[15]
         face them with Zen zazen[16] & tea
            made from the dust of the wings
               of butterflies dreaming
                    they're philosophers?

Or meet them with last war's tanks
  roaring out of Fort Ord[17]
   down the highways & canyons
    shooting as they come
flame-throwers flaming jelly
          into the Chinese rushes
          under the bridge at Bixby?
The U.S. owns the highway but is Big Sur
              in the USA?
    San Francisco floats away
    beyond the three-mile limit
 of the District of Eternal Revenue
    No need to pay your taxes
    The seas come in to cover us
  Agape we are & agape we'll be
              —San Francisco, June 22, 1966

[1]*Mt. Tamal-Fuji* Mt. Tamalpais, a mountain north of San Francisco and west across the bay from Berkeley shaped rather like Mt. Fuji. [2]*Voznesensky* Andrei Voznesensky, a contemporary Russian poet who has visited San Francisco. [3]*Gutenberg Galaxy* the title of a book by Marshall McLuhan (1962) and the general term for the world brought into being by Gutenberg's invention of movable type in the fifteenth century. [4]*Spengler* Oswald Spengler (1880-1936), German philosopher and author of a treatise entitled *The Decline of the West.* [5]*Gunga Din* title and character of a poem by Rudyard Kipling. [6]*Kipling* Rudyard Kipling (1865-1936), English poet who wrote in favor of the British Empire and who believed in the natural superiority of the white races. [7]*Merde* (French) "shit." [8]*Four Quartets* a series of poems by the Anglo-American poet T. S. Eliot (1888-1964). [9]*Anais Nin* American writer of experimental, avant-garde prose and of diaries. [10]*Virginia Woolf* English novelist and essayist (1882-1941). [11]*Big Sur* a stretch of beautiful, wild coastline in northern California. [12]*Kali* the Hindu goddess of destruction. [13]*koan* a short anecdote concerning the incomprehensible and illogical behavior and language of certain Zen masters; a subject for meditation (Gary Snyder's definition in *Earth House Hold,* p. 45). [14]*Ron Boise's lovers* the sculptor Ron Boise made a series of metal figures depicting all the positions of love. [15]*Kama Sutra* an ancient treatise written in Sanskrit on the subjects of love, marriage, and love-making. [16]*zazen* meditation. [17]*Fort Ord* an Army training camp on the California coast.

PETE SEEGER

Pete Seeger, musician, singer, and song writer, was born 1919, New York City, attended school at Avon Old Farms (Avon, Connecticut) and Harvard, and has spent much of his life collecting and singing traditional folk songs. In the forties he formed two singing groups—the Almanac Singers, with Woody Guthrie, and the Weavers. In the fifties the House Committee on Un-American Activities subpoenaed him to testify about "subversive" influences among singers and entertainers. Instead he cited the First Amendment provision for freedom of speech and association, refused to testify, and was found guilty of Contempt of Congress. His conviction was reversed in 1962. "Where Have All the Flowers Gone?" was inspired by a passage from Mikhail Sholokhov's novel *And Quiet Flows the Don.* It was recorded in 1961 on *Where Have All the Flowers Gone?* (Folkways FTS 31026).

WHERE HAVE ALL THE FLOWERS GONE?*

Where have all the flowers gone,
Long time passing?
Where have all the flowers gone,
Long time ago?
Where have all the flowers gone?
The girls have picked them every one.
    When will they ever learn?
    When will they ever learn?

Where have all the young girls gone,
Long time passing?
Where have all the young girls gone,
Long time ago?
Where have all the young girls gone?
They've taken husbands every one.
    When will they ever learn?
    When will they ever learn?

* © copyright 1961 by Fall River Music Inc. All rights reserved and used by permission of the Publisher.

Where have all the young men gone,
Long time passing?
Where have all the young men gone,
Long time ago?
Where have all the young men gone?
They're all in uniform.
    When will they ever learn?
    When will they ever learn?

Where have all the soldiers gone,
Long time passing?
Where have all the soldiers gone,
Long time ago?
Where have all the soldiers gone?
They've gone to graveyards, every one.
    When will they ever learn?
    O when will they ever learn?

Where have all the graveyards gone,
Long time passing?
Where have all the graveyards gone,
Long time ago?
Where have all the graveyards gone?
They're covered with flowers, every one.
    O when will they ever learn?
    O when will they ever learn?

Where have all the flowers gone,
Long time passing?
Where have all the flowers gone,
Long time ago?
Where have all the flowers gone?
Young girls picked them, every one.
    O when will they ever learn?
    O when will they ever learn?

ROBERT DUNCAN

Robert Duncan was born 1919 in Oakland, California, went to the University of California, Berkeley, and now lives in San Francisco where he shares a Victorian house with Jess Collins, a painter. He played a leading role in the "San Francisco Renaissance" of poetry in the late fifties. The poems are from *Roots and Branches* (1964) and *Bending the Bow* (1968).

Of poetry he has said:

A longing grows to return to the open composition in which the accidents and imperfections of speech might awake intimations of human being.

—"PAGES FROM A NOTEBOOK," IN DONALD M. ALLEN, ED., *The New American Poetry 1945-1960,* 1960

NEL MEZZO DEL CAMMIN DI NOSTRA VITA,[1]

at 42, Simon Rodilla, tile-setter,
    "to do something big for America" began
the Watts towers
(this year, 1959, the officials of which city
having initiated condemnation hearings
against which masterpiece)

               three spires
   rising 104 feet, bejewelld with glass,
shells, fragments of tile, scavenged
   from the city dump, from sea-wrack,
taller than the Holy Roman Catholic church
   steeples, and, moreover,
inspired; built up from bits of beauty
   sorted out—thirty-three years of it—
the great mitred structure rising
   out of squalid suburbs where the
mind is beaten back to the traffic, ground
   down to the drugstore, the mean regular houses
straggling out of downtown sections
   of imagination defeated. "They're
taller than the Church," he told us
   proudly.[2]

                    Art, dedicated to itself!

The cathedral at Palma too
        soard above church doctrine,
with art-nouveau windows and baldachine by Gaudi
        gatherd its children
under one roof of the imagination.

                        The poem . . .

"The poet,"
Charles Olson writes,
"cannot afford to traffic in any other *sign* than his one"
"his self," he says, "the man
or woman he is" Who? Rodia
        at 81 is through work.
Whatever man or woman he is,
        he is a tower, three towers,
a trinity upraised by himself.
        "Otherwise God does rush in."

Finisht.   "There are only his own
        composed forms, and each one
the issue of the time of the moment of its creation,
not any ultimate except what he in his heat
and that instant in its solidity yield";

like the Tower of Jewels at the San Francisco
        Panama-Pacific Exposition in 1915, this
"phantom kingdom to symbolize man's
        highest aims," glittering, but

an original, accretion of disregarded
        splendors
resurrected against the rules,
having in this its personal joke; its genius
        misfitting
the expected mediocre; an ecstasy
        of broken bottles
and colord dishes thrown up against whatever
        piety, city ordinance, plans,
risking height;

                    a fairy citadel,
a fabulous construction out of
        Christianity where Morgan le Fay[3]
carries the King to her enchanted Isle
        —all glass beads of many colors
and ricketty towers, concrete gardens,
        that imitate magnificence.

"Art," Burckhardt[4] writes:
"the most arrogant traitor of all
putting eyes and ears . . . in place of
        profounder worship"
"substituting figures for feelings."

        The rounds contain crowns.
        The increases climb by bridges.

        The whole
planned to occupy life and allow
        for death:

                    a skeletal remain
as glory, a raised image, sceptre,
        spectral island, most arrogant,
"to do something big for America"[5]

        Rodia.

[1]*Nel Mezzo del Cammin di Nostra Vita* The opening line of Dante's *The Divine Comedy.* The whole first stanza is as follows:
        Midway upon the road of our life
            I awoke to find myself in a dark wood,
                Where the right way was wholly lost and gone.
[2]The towers survived condemnation; they even survived the force of a hook attached to a truck pulling at them to bring them down. (The city argued they were an earthquake hazard.) They also survived the riots in Watts. Neighborhood groups have made of Rodilla's tiny house a sort of museum and neighborhood center. The towers, together with walls, fountains, and fantastic bridges decorated with bits of tile, bottles, and broken crockery, occupy the garden of Rodilla's house. Rodilla ("Rodia") is now dead. [3]*Morgan le Fay* sister of King Arthur and a sorceress; she is said in the tales of Arthur to have taken the dying king to an enchanted island from which he would one day return. [4]*Burckhardt* Jacob Burckhardt (1818-1897), historian of the art and culture of Renaissance Italy.
[5]*"to do something big for America"* Rodilla's words when interviewers asked him why he had built the towers.

ROBERT DUNCAN

THE MULTIVERSITY[1]   PASSAGES 21

       not men   but heads of the hydra
    his false faces in which
       authority lies
  hired minds of private interests
       over us

here: Kerr (behind him, heads of the Bank of America
            the Tribune,[2]
               heads of usury, heads of war)
    the worm's   mouthpiece   spreads
                    what it wishes   its own
false news[3]: 1) that the students broke into Sproul's office, vandalizing,
    creating disorder; 2) that the Free Speech Movement had no wide
    support, only an irresponsible minority going on strike
Chancellor Strong,   the dragon claw
        biting his bowels, his bile
    raging against the lawful demand
        for right reason.

In this scene   absolute authority
  the great dragon himself so confronted
  whose scales are men officized—ossified—conscience
      no longer alive in them,
  the inner law silenced,   now
        they call out their cops, police law,
        the club, the gun, the strong arm,
        gang-law of the state,
        hired sadists of installd mediocrities.

The aging Professor, translator of fashionable surrealist
    revolutionaries, muttering—

    *They shld not be permitted to be students; they shld
    be in the army.*

Where there is no commune,
        the individual volition has no ground.

             Where there is no individual freedom,   the commune
                    is falsified.

   in Blake's day   "old Nobodaddy"
                    in whose image, reduced in spirit
                        Kerr
(Stevenson, lying in the U.N. to save face)
                    He swore a great & solemn Oath
                    To kill the people I am loth.
                    But if they rebel, they must go to hell:
                    They shall have a Priest & a passing bell.

   muttering—
                "Theyv caused all this trouble in the South.   The responsible
            blacks dont want to have anything to do with them.   Now they are
            making trouble here.   But theyv been arrested and fingerprinted; we
            know who they are; we know how to stop them . . ."
                    Farted & belch'd & cough'd
                    And said, 'I love hanging & drawing & quartering
                    Every bit as well as war & slaughtering . . .

(in his first campaign, Stevenson, facing the Korean abattoir:
   "We will continue to pursue our peaceful purposes in Asia")

                    *Damn praying & singing
                    Unless they will bring in
                    The blood of ten thousand by fighting or swinging*

   3) that only some three hundred students are concernd
      about freedom of speech; only
         thirty, the hard core   [Kerr]
                                but behind them
        a hidden community,   three thousand
           outside the university in this
               conspiracy for free speech

    This wave will retreat and men will cease to care . . .

Each day   the last day;   each day   the
          beginning   the first word
                  door of the day or law awakening we create,
      vowels sung in a field in mid-morning
                  awakening the heart from its oppressions.

                                            ROBERT DUNCAN   79

Evil "referrd to the root of *up, over*"
simulacra of law that wld over-rule
    the Law man's inner nature seeks,

coils about them,   not men but
    heads and armors of the worm   office is

There being no common good, no commune,
no communion, outside the freedom of
        individual volition.

[1]*The Multiversity* Clark Kerr, president of the University of California from 1958 to 1965, coined this term to describe the modern university, open to society and in the service of society. [2]*the Tribune* The Oakland Tribune, a newspaper. [3]*false news* false news about the student demonstrators at Berkeley during 1964-1965. The activities of that academic year went by the name of the Free Speech Movement. In the fall of 1964 students who had spent the summer in the South organizing demonstrations against practices of racial segregation returned to Berkeley, where they began to organize demonstrations against local employers, among them the Bank of America, which, they said, practiced discrimination in hiring.

JAMES DICKEY

James Dickey (born 1923, Atlanta, Georgia; attended Clemson College and Vanderbilt) had a career in advertising before he began to give most of his time to poetry. He flew in the Air Corps during World War II and in the Air Force during the Korean War. He is a novelist *(Deliverance)* as well as a poet. He lives in Columbia, South Carolina. "Cherrylog Road" is from *Helmets* (1964).

CHERRYLOG ROAD

Off Highway 106
At Cherrylog Road I entered
The '34 Ford without wheels,
Smothered in kudzu,
With a seat pulled out to run
Corn whiskey down from the hills,

And then from the other side
Crept into an Essex
With a rumble seat of red leather
And then out again, aboard
A blue Chevrolet, releasing
The rust from its other color,

Reared up on three building blocks.
None had the same body heat;
I changed with them inward, toward
The weedy heart of the junkyard,
For I knew that Doris Holbrook
Would escape from her father at noon

And would come from the farm
To seek parts owned by the sun
Among the abandoned chassis,
Sitting in each in turn
As I did, leaning forward
As in a wild stock-car race

In the parking lot of the dead.
Time after time, I climbed in
And out the other side, like
An envoy or movie star
Met at the station by crickets.
A radiator cap raised its head,

Become a real toad or a kingsnake
As I neared the hub of the yard,
Passing through many states,
Many lives, to reach
Some grandmother's long Pierce-Arrow
Sending platters of blindness forth

From its nickel hubcaps
And spilling its tender upholstery
On sleepy roaches,
The glass panel in between
Lady and colored driver
Not all the way broken out,

The back-seat phone
Still on its hook.
I got in as though to exclaim,
"Let us go to the orphan asylum,
John; I have some old toys
For children who say their prayers."

I popped with sweat as I thought
I heard Doris Holbrook scrape
Like a mouse in the southern-state sun
That was eating the paint in blisters
From a hundred car tops and hoods.
She was tapping like code,

Loosening the screws,
Carrying off headlights,
Sparkplugs, bumpers,
Cracked mirrors and gear-knobs,
Getting ready, already,
To go back with something to show

Other than her lips' new trembling
I would hold to me soon, soon,
Where I sat in the ripped back seat
Talking over the interphone,
Praying for Doris Holbrook
To come from her father's farm

And to get back there
With no trace of me on her face
To be seen by her red-haired father
Who would change, in the squalling barn,
Her back's pale skin with a strop,
Then lay for me

In a bootlegger's roasting car
With a string-triggered 12-gauge shotgun
To blast the breath from the air.
Not cut by the jagged windshields,
Through the acres of wrecks she came
With a wrench in her hand,

Through dust where the blacksnake dies
Of boredom, and the beetle knows
The compost has no more life.
Someone outside would have seen
The oldest car's door inexplicably
Close from within:

I held her and held her and held her,
Convoyed at terrific speed
By the stalled, dreaming traffic around us,
So the blacksnake, stiff
With inaction, curved back
Into life, and hunted the mouse

With deadly overexcitement,
The beetles reclaimed their field
As we clung, glued together,
With the hooks of the seat springs
Working through to catch us red-handed
Amidst the gray breathless batting

That burst from the seat at our backs.
We left by separate doors
Into the changed, other bodies
Of cars, she down Cherrylog Road
And I to my motorcycle
Parked like the soul of the junkyard

Restored, a bicycle fleshed
With power, and tore off
Up Highway 106, continually
Drunk on the wind in my mouth,
Wringing the handlebar for speed,
Wild to be wreckage forever.

DENISE LEVERTOV

Denise Levertov was born 1923 in Ilford, Essex (England) and educated at home by her clergyman father, a Russian Jew who had become a convert to the Anglican church, and her Welsh mother. She grew up in London and now lives in New York City. Her husband, Mitchell Goodman, an essayist and novelist, was indicted with Dr. Benjamin Spock and others for conspiring to counsel young men to resist the draft. The poems come from O Taste and See (1964).

HYPOCRITE WOMEN

Hypocrite women, how seldom we speak
of our own doubts, while dubiously
we mother man in his doubt!

And if at Mill Valley[1] perched in the trees
the sweet rain drifting through western air
a white sweating bull of a poet told us

our cunts are ugly—why didn't we
admit we have thought so too? (And
what shame? They are not for the eye!)

No, they are dark and wrinkled and hairy,
caves of the Moon . . .   And when a
dark humming fills us, a

coldness towards life,
we are too much women to
own to such unwomanliness.

Whorishly with the psychopomp
we play and plead—and say
nothing of this later.   And our dreams,

with that frivolity we have pared them
like toenails, clipped them like ends of
split hair.

[1] *Mill Valley* town north of San Francisco.

WHAT WERE THEY LIKE?

(Questions and Answers)

1) Did the people of Viet Nam
    use lanterns of stone?
2) Did they hold ceremonies
    to reverence the opening of buds?
3) Were they inclined to rippling laughter?
4) Did they use bone and ivory,
    jade and silver, for ornament?
5) Had they an epic poem?
6) Did they distinguish between speech and singing?

1) Sir, their light hearts turned to stone.
    It is not remembered whether in gardens
    stone lanterns illumined pleasant ways.
2) Perhaps they gathered once to delight in blossom,
    but after the children were killed
    there were no more buds.
3) Sir, laughter is bitter to the burned mouth.
4) A dream ago, perhaps. Ornament is for joy.
    All the bones were charred.
5) It is not remembered. Remember,
    most were peasants; their life
    was in rice and bamboo.
    When peaceful clouds were reflected in the paddies
    and the water-buffalo stepped surely along terraces,
    maybe fathers told their sons old tales.
    When bombs smashed the mirrors
    there was time only to scream.
6) There is an echo yet, it is said,
    of their speech which was like a song.
    It is reported their singing resembled
    the flight of moths in moonlight.
    Who can say? It is silent now.

DENISE LEVERTOV

JAMES SCHUYLER

James Schuyler (1923, Chicago) is a staff member of the Museum of Modern Art in New York. He attended Bethany College (West Virginia) and lived for several years in Italy; he now lives in Southhampton, New York. He is an author of prose fictions and off-Broadway plays. In collaboration with John Ashbery he wrote a novel-like fiction, *A Nest of Ninnies* (1969). The poems are from *Freely Espousing* (1969).

WITH FRANK AND GEORGE AT LEXINGTON

Polly Red Top Thermos is with us
and my 75-pound Flip-It pen
no lighter than our heads
on the rocks
among the shrinking snow.

Is this lichen, this stuff here?
And these leaves,
are they oak leaves,
and what can I read
in char, such as: black branch
were you a dogwood tree?
I feel it was, though.

The snow has footsteps in it
like wet cement; a cowlick
is in a tuft of last year's grass;
cars fly by like bees; and so on.
A big quill hat bends an evergreen
introspectively down.

It feels good here.

POEM

How about an oak leaf
if you had to be a leaf?
Suppose you had your life to live over
knowing what you know?
Suppose you had plenty money

"Get away from me you little fool."

Evening of a day in early March,
you are like the smell of drains
in a restaurant where paté maison
is a slab of cold meat loaf
damp and wooly. You lack charm.

3/23/66

It's funny early spring weather, mild and washy
the color of a head cold.
The air rushes. Branches
are going nowhere, like the ocean,
spring salt unstopping sinuses. Winter salt doesn't.
Everything just sitting around: a barn without eaves,
a dumpy cottage set catty-corner
on its lot, a field with a horse in it.
A plane goes over, leaving its wake,
an awakening snore. A truck
passes, perceived as a quick shuffle
of solitaire cards. And the poor old humpy lawn
is tufted with Irish eyebrows of onion grass.
A chill on the nape smells frowsty
the spring no more awake
than a first morning stretch
and no more asleep. Growing
and going, in sight and sound, as the fire last night
looked out at us reading *Great Expectations* aloud
and fled up the chimney.

EDWARD FIELD

Edward Field (1924, Brooklyn, attended New York University) has acted in summer circuit and off-Broadway theatre. He wrote the narration for the prize-winning film *To Be Alive*, which was shown at the Johnson's Wax Pavilion during the New York World's Fair. In 1962 he won a Lamont award for his poetry. He lives in New York City.

GRAFFITI

Blessings on all the kids who improve the signs in the subways:
They put a beard on the fashionable lady selling soap,
Fix up her flat chest with the boobies of a chorus girl,
And though her hips be wrapped like a mummy
They draw a hairy cunt where she should have one.

The bathing beauty who looks pleased
With the enormous prick in her mouth, declares
"Eat hair pie; it's better than cornflakes."
And the little boy in the tarzan suit eating white bread
Now has a fine pair of balls to crow about.

And as often as you wash the walls and put up your posters,
When you go back to the caged booth to deal out change
The bright-eyed kids will come with grubby hands.
Even if you watch, you cannot watch them all the time,
And while you are dreaming, if you have dreams anymore,

A boy and girl are giggling behind an iron pillar;
And although the train pulls in and takes them on their way
Into a winter that will freeze them forever,
They leave behind a wall scrawled all over with flowers
That shoot great drops of gism through the sky.

UNWANTED

The poster with my picture on it
Is hanging on the bulletin board in the Post Office.

I stand by it hoping to be recognized
Posing first full face and then profile

But everybody passes by and I have to admit
The photograph was taken some years ago.

I was unwanted then and I'm unwanted now
Ah guess ah'll go up echo mountain and crah.

I wish someone would find my fingerprints somewhere
Maybe on a corpse and say, You're it.

Description: Male, or reasonably so
White, but not lily-white and usually deep-red

Thirty-fivish, and looks it lately
Five-feet-nine and one-hundred-thirty pounds: no physique

Black hair going gray, hairline receding fast
What used to be curly, now fuzzy

Brown eyes starey under beetling brow
Mole on chin, probably will become a wen

It is perfectly obvious that he was not popular at school
No good at baseball, and wet his bed.

His aliases tell his history: Dumbell, Good-for-nothing,
Jewboy, Fieldinsky, Skinny, Fierce Face, Greaseball, Sissy.

Warning: This man is not dangerous, answers to any name
Responds to love, don't call him or he will come.

FRANKENSTEIN

The monster has escaped from the dungeon
where he was kept by the Baron,
who made him with knobs sticking out from each side of his neck
where the head was attached to the body
and stitching all over
where parts of cadavers were sewed together.

He is pursued by the ignorant villagers,
who think he is evil and dangerous because he is ugly
and makes ugly noises.
They wave firebrands at him and cudgels and rakes,
but he escapes and comes to the thatched cottage
of an old blind man playing on the violin Mendelssohn's "Spring Song."

Hearing him approach, the blind man welcomes him:
"Come in, my friend," and takes him by the arm.
"You must be weary," and sits him down inside the house.
For the blind man has long dreamed of having a friend
to share his lonely life.

The monster has never known kindness—the Baron was cruel—
but somehow he is able to accept it now,
and he really has no instincts to harm the old man,
for in spite of his awful looks he has a tender heart:
Who knows what cadaver that part of him came from?

The old man seats him at table, offers him bread,
and says, "Eat, my friend." The monster
rears back roaring in terror.
"No, my friend, it is good. Eat—gooood"
and the old man shows him how to eat,
and reassured, the monster eats
and says, "Eat—gooood,"
trying out the words and finding them good too.

The old man offers him a glass of wine,
"Drink, my friend. Drink—gooood."
The monster drinks, slurping horribly, and says,
"Drink—gooood," in his deep nutty voice
and smiles maybe for the first time in his life.

Then the blind man puts a cigar in the monster's mouth
and lights a large wooden match that flares up in his face.
The monster, remembering the torches of the villagers,
recoils, grunting in terror.
"No, my friend, smoke—gooood,"
and the old man demonstrates with his own cigar.
The monster takes a tentative puff
and smiles hugely, saying, "Smoke—gooood,"
and sits back like a banker, grunting and puffing.

Now the old man plays Mendelssohn's "Spring Song" on the violin
while tears come into our dear monster's eyes
as he thinks of the stones of the mob, the pleasures of mealtime,
the magic new words he has learned
and above all of the friend he has found.

It is just as well that he is unaware—
being simple enough to believe only in the present—
that the mob will find him and pursue him
for the rest of his short unnatural life,
until trapped at the whirlpool's edge
he plunges to his death.

THE BRIDE OF FRANKENSTEIN

The Baron has decided to mate the monster,
to breed him perhaps,
in the interests of pure science, his only god.

So he goes up into his laboratory
which he has built in the tower of the castle
to be as near the interplanetary forces as possible,
and puts together the prettiest monster-woman you ever saw
with a body like a pin-up girl
and hardly any stitching at all
where he sewed on the head of a raped and murdered beauty queen.

He sets his liquids burping, and coils blinking and buzzing,
and waits for an electric storm to send through the equipment
the spark vital for life.
The storm breaks over the castle
and the equipment really goes crazy
like a kitchen full of modern appliances
as the lightning juice starts oozing right into that pretty corpse.

He goes to get the monster
so he will be right there when she opens her eyes,
for she might fall in love with the first thing she sees as ducklings do.
That monster is already straining at his chains and slurping,
ready to go right to it:
He has been well prepared for coupling
by his pinching leering keeper who's been saying for weeks,
"Ya gonna get a little nookie, kid,"
or "How do you go for some poontang, baby?"
All the evil in him is focused on this one thing now
as he is led into her very presence.

She awakens slowly,
she bats her eyes,
she gets up out of the equipment,
and finally she stands in all her seamed glory,
a monster princess with a hairdo like a fright wig,
lighting flashing in the background
like a halo and a wedding veil,
like a photographer snapping pictures of great moments.

She stands and stares with her electric eyes,
beginning to understand that in this life too
she was just another body to be raped.

The monster is ready to go:
He roars with joy at the sight of her,
so they let him loose and he goes right for those knockers.
And she starts screaming to break your heart
and you realize that she was just born:
In spite of her big tits she was just a baby.

But her instincts are right—
rather death than that green slobber:
She jumps off the parapet.
And then the monster's sex drive goes wild.
Thwarted, it turns to violence, demonstrating sublimation crudely;
and he wrecks the lab, those burping acids and buzzing coils,
overturning the control panel so the equipment goes off like a bomb,
and the stone castle crumbles and crashes in the storm
destroying them all . . . perhaps.

Perhaps somehow the Baron got out of that wreckage of his dreams
with his evil intact, if not his good looks,
and more wicked than ever went on with his thrilling career.

And perhaps even the monster lived
to roam the earth, his desire still ungratified;
and lovers out walking in shadowy and deserted places
will see his shape loom up over them, their doom—
and children sleeping in their beds
will wake up in the dark night screaming
as his hideous body grabs them.

THE RETURN OF FRANKENSTEIN

He didn't die in the whirlpool by the mill
where he had fallen in after a wild chase
by all the people of the town.

Somehow he clung to an overhanging rock
until the villagers went away.

And when he came out, he was changed forever,
that soft heart of his had hardened
and he really was a monster now.

He was out to pay them back,
to throw the lie of brotherly love
in their white Christian teeth.

Wasn't his flesh human flesh
even made from the bodies of criminals,
the worst the Baron could find?

But love is not necessarily implicit in human flesh:
Their hatred was now his hatred,

so he set out on his new career
his previous one being the victim,
the good man who suffers.

Now no longer the hunted but the hunter
he was in charge of his destiny
and knew how to be cold and clever,

preserving barely a spark of memory
for the old blind musician
who once took him in and offered brotherhood.

His idea—if his career now had an idea—
was to kill them all,
keep them in terror anyway,
let them feel hunted.
Then perhaps they would look at others
with a little pity and love.

Only a suffering people have any virtue.

KENNETH KOCH

Kenneth Koch was born in 1925 in Cincinnati, Ohio. He went to Harvard and Columbia, and he now teaches at Columbia. He has written plays for the off-Broadway and off-off-Broadway theatre.

FRESH AIR

I

At the Poem Society a black-haired man stands up to say
"You make me sick with all your talk about restraint and mature talent!
Haven't you ever looked out the window at a painting by Matisse,
Or did you always stay in hotels where there were too many spiders crawling on your visages?
Did you ever glance inside a bottle of sparkling pop,
Or see a citizen split in two by the lightning?
I am afraid you have never smiled at the hibernation
Of bear cubs except that you saw in it some deep relation
To human suffering and wishes, oh what a bunch of crackpots!"
The black-haired man sits down, and the others shoot arrows at him.
A blond man stands up and says,
"He is right! Why should we be organized to defend the kingdom
Of dullness? There are so many slimy people connected with poetry,
Too, and people who know nothing about it!
I am not recommending that poets like each other and organize to fight them,
But simply that lightning should strike them."
Then the assembled mediocrities shot arrows at the blond-haired man.
The chairman stood up on the platform, oh he was physically ugly!
He was small-limbed and -boned and thought he was quite seductive,
But he was bald with certain hideous black hairs,
And his voice had the sound of water leaving a vaseline bathtub,
And he said, "The subject for this evening's discussion is poetry
On the subject of love between swans." And everyone threw candy hearts
At the disgusting man, and they stuck to his bib and tucker,
And he danced up and down on the platform in terrific glee
And recited the poetry of his little friends—but the blond man stuck his head

Out of a cloud and recited poems about the east and thunder,
And the black-haired man moved through the stratosphere chanting
Poems of the relationships between terrific prehistoric charcoal whales,
And the slimy man with candy hearts sticking all over him
Wilted away like a cigarette paper on which the bumblebees have urinated,
And all the professors left the room to go back to their duty,
And all that were left in the room were five or six poets
And together they sang the new poem of the twentieth century
Which, though influenced by Mallarmé, Shelley, Byron, and Whitman,
Plus a million other poets, is still entirely original
And is so exciting that it cannot be here repeated.
You must go to the Poem Society and wait for it to happen.
Once you have heard this poem you will not love any other,
Once you have dreamed this dream you will be inconsolable,
Once you have loved this dream you will be as one dead,
Once you have visited the passages of this time's great art!

II

"Oh to be seventeen years old
Once again," sang the red-haired man, "and not know that poetry
Is ruled with the sceptre of the dumb, the deaf, and the creepy!"
And the shouting persons battered his immortal body with stones
And threw his primitive comedy into the sea
From which it sang forth poems irrevocably blue.

Who are the great poets of our time, and what are their names?
Yeats of the baleful influence, Auden of the baleful influence, Eliot of the baleful influence
(Is Eliot a great poet? no one knows), Hardy, Stevens, Williams (is Hardy of our time?),
Hopkins (is Hopkins of our time?), Rilke (is Rilke of our time?), Lorca (is Lorca of our time?), who is still of our time?
Mallarmé, Valéry, Apollinaire, Eluard, Reverdy, French poets are still of our time,
Pasternak and Mayakovsky, is Jouve of our time?

Where are young poets in America, they are trembling in publishing houses and universities,
Above all they are trembling in universities, they are bathing the library steps with their spit,

KENNETH KOCH 97

They are gargling out innocuous (to whom?) poems about maple trees and their children,
Sometimes they brave a subject like the Villa d'Este or a lighthouse in Rhode Island,
Oh what worms they are! they wish to perfect their form.

Yet could not these young men, put in another profession,
Succeed admirably, say at sailing a ship? I do not doubt it, Sir, and I wish we could try them.
(A plane flies over the ship holding a bomb but perhaps it will not drop the bomb,
The young poets from the universities are staring anxiously at the skies,
Oh they are remembering their days on the campus when they looked up to watch birds excrete,
They are remembering the days they spent making their elegant poems.)
Is there no voice to cry out from the wind and say what it is like to be the wind,
To be roughed up by the trees and to bring music from the scattered houses
And the stones, and to be in such intimate relationship with the sea
That you cannot understand it? Is there no one who feels like a pair of pants?

III

Summer in the trees! "It is time to strangle several bad poets."
The yellow hobbyhorse rocks to and fro, and from the chimney
Drops the Strangler! The white and pink roses are slightly agitated by the struggle,
But afterwards beside the dead "poet" they cuddle up comfortingly against their vase. They are safer now, no one will compare them to the sea.

Here on the railroad train, one more time, is the Strangler.
He is going to get that one there, who is on his way to a poetry reading.
Agh! Biff! A body falls to the moving floor.

In the football stadium I also see him,
He leaps through the frosty air at the maker of comparisons
Between football and life and silently, silently strangles him!

Here is the Strangler dressed in a cowboy suit
Leaping from his horse to annihilate the students of myth!

The Strangler's ear is alert for the names of Orpheus,
Cuchulain, Gawain, and Odysseus,
And for poems addressed to Jane Austen, F. Scott Fitzgerald,
To Ezra Pound, and to personages no longer living
Even in anyone's thoughts—O Strangler the Strangler!
He lies on his back in the waves of the Pacific Ocean.

IV

Supposing that one walks out into the air
On a fresh spring day and has the misfortune
To encounter an article on modern poetry
In *New World Writing*, or has the misfortune
To see some examples of some of the poetry
Written by the men with their eyes on the myth
And the Missus and the midterms, in the *Hudson Review*,
Or, if one is abroad, in *Botteghe Oscure*,
Or indeed in *Encounter*, what is one to do
With the rest of one's day that lies blasted to ruins
All bluely about one, what is one to do?
O surely one cannot complain to the President,
Nor even to the deans of Columbia College,
Nor to T. S. Eliot, nor to Ezra Pound,
And supposing one writes to the Princess Caetani,
"Your poets are awful!" what good would it do?
And supposing one goes to the *Hudson Review*
With a package of matches and sets fire to the building?
One ends up in prison with trial subscriptions
To the *Partisan, Sewanee,* and *Kenyon Review!*

V

Sun out! perhaps there is a reason for the lack of poetry
In these ill-contented souls, perhaps they need air!

Blue air, fresh air, come in, I welcome you, you are an art student,
Take off your cap and gown and sit down on the chair.
Together we shall paint the poets—but no, air! perhaps you should go
    to them, quickly,
Give them a little inspiration, they need it, perhaps they are out of
    breath,
Give them a little inhuman company before they freeze the English
    language to death!

(And rust their typewriters a little, be sea air! be noxious! kill them,
    if you must, but stop their poetry!
I remember I saw you dancing on the surf on the Côte d'Azur,
And I stopped, taking my hat off, but you did not remember me,
Then afterwards you came to my room bearing a handful of orange
    flowers
And we were together all through the summer night!)

That we might go away together, it is so beautiful on the sea, there
    are a few white clouds in the sky!

But no, air! you must go . . . Ah, stay!

But she has departed and . . . Ugh! what poisonous fumes and clouds!
    what a suffocating atmosphere!
Cough! whose are these hideous faces I see, what is this rigor
Infecting the mind? where are the green Azores,
Fond memories of childhood, and the pleasant orange trolleys,
A girl's face, red-white, and her breasts and calves, blue eyes, brown
    eyes, green eyes, fahrenheit
Temperatures, dandelions, and trains, O blue?!
Wind, wind, what is happening? Wind! I can't see any bird but the
    gull, and I feel it should symbolize . . .
Oh, pardon me, there's a swan, one two three swans, a great white
    swan, hahaha how pretty they are! Smack!
Oh! stop! help! yes, I see—disrespect of my superiors—forgive me, dear
    Zeus, nice Zeus, parabolic bird, O feathered excellence! white!
There is Achilles too, and there's Ulysses, I've always wanted to see
    them, hahaha!
And there is Helen of Troy, I suppose she is Zeus too, she's so terribly
    pretty—hello, Zeus, my you are beautiful, Bang!
One more mistake and I get thrown out of the Modern Poetry Association,
    help! Why aren't there any adjectives around?
Oh there are, there's practically nothing else—look, here's *grey, utter,
    agonized, total, phenomenal, gracile, invidious, sundered,* and *fused,*
Elegant, absolute, pyramidal, and . . . Scream! but what can I describe with
    these words? States!
States symbolized and divided by two, complex states, magic states, states
    of consciousness governed by an aroused sincerity, cockadoodle doo!
Another bird! is it morning? Help! where am I? am I in the barnyard?
    oink oink, scratch, moo! Splash!
My first lesson. "Look around you. What do you think and feel?" *Uhhh
    . . . "Quickly!" This Connecticut landscape would have pleased Vermeer.*

Wham! A-Plus.

"Congratulations!" I am promoted.

OOOhhhhh I wish I were dead, what a headache! My second lesson: "Rewrite your first lesson line six hundred times. Try to make it into a magnetic field." I can do it too. But my poor line! What a nightmare! Here comes a tremendous horse,

Trojan, I presume. No, it's my third lesson. "Look, look! Watch him, see what he's doing? That's what we want you to do. Of course it won't be the same as his at first, but . . ." I demur. Is there no other way to fertilize minds?

Bang! I give in . . . Already I see my name in two or three anthologies, a serving girl comes into the barn bringing me the anthologies,

She is very pretty and I smile at her a little sadly, perhaps it is my last smile! Perhaps she will hit me! But no, she smiles in return, and she takes my hand.

My hand, my hand! what is this strange thing I feel in my hand, on my arm, on my chest, my face—can it be . . . ? it is! AIR!

Air, air, you've come back! Did you have any success? "What do you think." I don't know, air. You are so strong, air.

And she breaks my chains of straw, and we walk down the road, behind us the hideous fumes!

Soon we reach the seaside, she is a young art student who places her head on my shoulder,

I kiss her warm red lips, and here is the Strangler, reading the *Kenyon Review!* Good luck to you, Strangler!

Goodbye, Helen! goodbye, fumes! goodbye, abstracted dried-up boys! goodbye, dead trees! goodbye, skunks!

Goodbye, manure! goodbye, critical manicure! goodbye, you big fat men standing on the east coast as well as the west giving poems the test! farewell, Valéry's stern dictum!

Until tomorrow, then, scum floating on the surface of poetry! goodbye for a moment, refuse that happens to land in poetry's boundaries! adieu, stale eggs teaching imbeciles poetry to bolster up your egos! adios, boring anomalies of these same stale eggs!

Ah, but the scum is deep! Come, let me help you! and soon we pass into the clear blue water. Oh GOODBYE, castrati of poetry! farewell, stale pale skunky pentameters (the only honest English meter, gloop gloop!) until tomorrow, horrors! oh, farewell!

Hello, sea! good morning, sea! hello, clarity and excitement, you great expanse of green—

O green, beneath which all of them shall drown!

BOB KAUFMAN

Bob Kaufman's poems have been translated into Italian, French, and Spanish, but he has not been widely read in his own country. Born in 1925 in New Orleans, Louisiana, in the fifties, he was a founder of *Beatitude* magazine in San Francisco, where he now lives. For some twenty years a merchant seaman, he began as a cabin boy at thirteen. The poems are from *Solitudes Crowded with Loneliness* (1965) and *Golden Sardine* (1967).

PLEA

Voyager, wanderer of the heart,
Off to
          a million midnights, black, black
Voyager, wanderer of star worlds,
Off to
          a million tomorrows, black, black,
Seek and find Hiroshima's children,
          Send them back, send them back.
Tear open concrete sealed cathedrals, spiritually locked
          Fill vacant theaters with their musty diversions,
Almost forgotten laughter.

Give us back the twisted sons
Poisoned by mildewed fathers.
Find again the used up whores,
Dying in some forgotten corner,
Find sunlight, and barking dogs,
For the lost, decayed in sorry jails.
Find pity, find Hell for wax bitches,
Hidden in the bowels of male Cadillacs.
Find tomorrow and next time for Negro millionaires
Hopelessly trapped in their luxurious complexions.
Find love, and an everlasting fix for hopeless junkies,
Stealing into lost nights, long time.

Voyager now,
           Off to a million midnights, black, black
Seek and find Hiroshima's children,
           Send them back, send them back.

JAIL POEMS

1

I am sitting in a cell with a view of evil parallels,
Waiting thunder to splinter me into a thousand me's.
It is not enough to be in one cage with one self;
I want to sit opposite every prisoner in every hole.
Doors roll and bang, every slam a finality, bang!
The junkie disappeared into a red noise, stoning out his hell.
The odored wino congratulates himself on not smoking,
Fingerprints left lying on black inky gravestones,
Noises of pain seeping through steel walls crashing
Reach my own hurt. I become part of someone forever.
Wild accents of criminals are sweeter to me than hum of cops,
Busy battening down hatches of human souls; cargo
Destined for ports of accusations, harbors of guilt.
What do policemen eat, Socrates, still prisoner, old one?

2

Painter, paint me a crazy jail, mad water-color cells.
Poet, how old is suffering? Write it in yellow lead.
God, make me a sky on my glass ceiling. I need stars now,
To lead through this atmosphere of shrieks and private hells,
Entrances and exits, in . . . out . . . up . . . down, the civic seesaw.
Here—me—now—hear—me—now—always here somehow.

3

In a universe of cells—who is not in jail? Jailers.
In a world of hospitals—who is not sick? Doctors.
A golden sardine is swimming in my head.
Oh we know some things, man, about some things
Like jazz and jails and God.
Saturday is a good day to go to jail.

4

Now they give a new form, quivering jelly-like,
That proves any boy can be president of Muscatel.
They are mad at him because he's one of Them.
Gray-speckled unplanned nakedness; stinking
Fingers grasping toilet bowl. Mr. America wants to bathe.
Look! On the floor, lying across America's face—
A real movie star featured in a million newsreels.
What am I doing—feeling compassion?
When he comes out of it, he will help kill me.
He probably hates living.

5

Nuts, skin bolts, clanking in his stomach, scrambled.
His society's gone to pieces in his belly, bloated.
See the great American windmill, tilting at itself,
Good solid stock, the kind that made America drunk.
Success written all over his street-streaked ass.
Successful-type success, forty home runs in one inning.
Stop suffering, Jack, you can't fool us. We know.
This is the greatest country in the world, ain't it?
He didn't make it. Wino in Cell 3.

6

There have been too many years in this short span of mine.
My soul demands a cave of its own, like the Jain god;
Yet I must make it go on, hard like jazz, glowing
In this dark plastic jungle, land of long night, chilled.
My navel is a button to push when I want inside out.
Am I not more than a mass of entrails and rough tissue?
Must I break my bones? Drink my wine-diluted blood?
Should I dredge old sadness from my chest?
Not again.
All those ancient balls of fire, hotly swallowed, let them lie.
Let me spit breath mists of introspection, bits of me,
So that when I am gone, I shall be in the air.

7

Someone whom I am is no one.
Something I have done is nothing.
Someplace I have been is nowhere.

I am not me.
What of the answers
I must find questions for?
All these strange streets
I must find cities for,
Thank God for beatniks.

8

All night the stink of rotting people,
Fumes rising from pyres of live men,
Fill my nose with gassy disgust,
Drown my exposed eyes in tears.

9

Traveling God salesmen, bursting my ear drum
With the dullest part of a good sexy book,
Impatient for Monday and adding machines.

10

Yellow-eyed dogs whistling in evening.

11

The baby came to jail today.

12

One more day to hell, filled with floating glands.

13

The jail, a huge hollow metal cube
Hanging from the moon by a silver chain.
Someday Johnny Appleseed is going to chop it down.

14

Three long strings of light
Braided into a ray.

15

I am apprehensive about my future;
My past has turned its back on me.

16

Shadows I see, forming on the wall,
Pictures of desires protected from my own eyes.

17

After spending all night constructing a dream,
Morning came and blinded me with light.
Now I seek among mountains of crushed eggshells
For the God damned dream I never wanted.

18

Sitting here writing things on paper,
Instead of sticking the pencil into the air.

19

The Battle of Monumental Failures raging,
Both hoping for a good clean loss.

20

Now I see the night, silently overwhelming day.

21

Caught in imaginary webs of conscience,
I weep over my acts, yet believe.

22

Cities should be built on one side of the street.

23

People who can't cast shadows
Never die of freckles.

24

The end always comes last.

25

We sat at a corner table,
Devouring each other word by word,
Until nothing was left, repulsive skeletons.

26

I sit here writing, not daring to stop,
For fear of seeing what's outside my head.

27

There, Jesus, didn't hurt a bit, did it?

28

I am afraid to follow my flesh over those narrow
Wide hard soft female beds, but I do.

29

Link by link, we forged the chain.
Then, discovering the end around our necks,
We bugged out.

30

I have never seen a wild poetic loaf of bread,
But if I did, I would eat it, crust and all.

31

From how many years away does a baby come?

32

Universality, duality, totality . . . one.

33

The defective on the floor, mumbling,
Was once a man who shouted across tables.

34

Come, help flatten a raindrop.
    —Written in San Francisco City Prison Cell 3, 1959

A SUPERMARKET IN CALIFORNIA

What thoughts I have of you tonight, Walt Whitman, for I walked down the sidestreets under the trees with a headache self-conscious looking at the full moon.

In my hungry fatigue, and shopping for images, I went into the neon fruit supermarket, dreaming of your enumerations!

What peaches and what penumbras! Whole families shopping at night! Aisles full of husbands! Wives in the avocados, babies in the tomatoes! — and you, García Lorca, what were you doing down by the watermelons?

I saw you, Walt Whitman, childless, lonely old grubber, poking among the meats in the refrigerator and eyeing the grocery boys.

I heard you asking questions of each: Who killed the pork chops? What price bananas? Are you my Angel?

I wandered in and out of the brilliant stacks of cans following you, and followed in my imagination by the store detective.

We strode down the open corridors together in our solitary fancy tasting artichokes, possessing every frozen delicacy, and never passing the cashier.

Where are we going, Walt Whitman? The doors close in an hour. Which way does your beard point tonight?

(I touch your book and dream of our odyssey in the supermarket and feel absurd.)

Will we walk all night through solitary streets? The trees add shade to shade, lights out in the houses, we'll both be lonely.

Will we stroll dreaming of the lost America of love past blue automobiles in driveways, home to our silent cottage?

Ah, dear father, graybeard, lonely old courage-teacher, what America did you have when Charon quit poling his ferry and you got out on a smoking bank and stood watching the boat disappear on the black waters of Lethe?

—Allen Ginsberg

ALLEN GINSBERG

Q. Will you please state your full name?
A. Allen Ginsberg.
Q. What is your occupation?
A. Poet.
Q. Have you authored any books in the field of poetry?
A. Yes.
Q. Will you indicate to the jury the titles of the books you have authored?
A. In 1956, *Howl and Other Poems;* in 1960, *Kaddish and Other Poems;* in 1963, *Empty Mirror;* in 1963, *Reality Sandwiches;* and in 1968, *Planet News.*
Q. Now, in addition to your writing, Mr. Ginsberg, are you presently engaged in any other activities?
A. I teach, lecture, and recite poetry at universities. . . .
Q. Would you describe for the court and jury what the Be-In in San Francisco was? . . .
A. A gathering together of younger people aware of the planetary fate that we are all sitting in the middle of, imbued with a new consciousness and desiring of a new kind of society involving prayer, music, and spiritual life together rather than competition and war.*

This is the beginning of Allen Ginsberg's testimony at the conspiracy trial of the "Chicago Eight," those radical individuals charged in 1969 with bringing violence to the 1968 Democratic National Convention in Chicago. Ginsberg also chanted and recited poetry at that trial. He spoke reverently of his spiritual forebears, William Blake and Walt Whitman. He patiently explained the religious significance of his poems to an exasperated prosecutor. He described his own unconscious tendencies to love humanity as "charming." Upon the completion of his testimony, half the court rose in tribute to him.

No American poet of today has so fully sustained the prophetic style as Ginsberg. He is at once the teacher, the permanent rebel, the guru, the happy leader of enlightened humanity, the blissful fool, the reconciler of differences, the promoter of both himself and wisdom. Asked once (by the editor of a reference work on contemporary poets) to comment on his achievement, he replied: "I have achieved the introduction of the word *fuck* into texts inevitably studied by schoolboys."*

---

*Quoted from an abridged transcript of Ginsberg's testimony in *The Movement Toward a New America,* assembled by Mitchell Goodman (Philadelphia: Pilgrim Press, and New York: Alfred A. Knopf, 1970), p. [566].

*Rosalie Murphy, ed., *Contemporary Poets of the English Language* (Chicago and London: St. James Press, 1970).

So much for the notorious side of his success. The popular press, which made so much of the "beats" in the fifties and of the "hippies" in the sixties, has always been amused or scandalized (often both) by the freakishness of Ginsberg and his curious friends, among them the novelists Jack Kerouac and Ken Kesey, the poet Peter Orlovsky, and the Zen mystic and poet Gary Snyder. But there is another important side to Ginsberg, a side that is revealed when he speaks about the rhythmic techniques of his poetry. Then he is the brilliant Columbia student, the scholar: "They're probably more choriambic—Greek meters, dithyrambic meters—and tending toward de DA de de DA de de . . . what is that? Tending toward dactylic, probably. [William Carlos] Williams once remarked that American speech tends toward dactylic."* Both poets of New Jersey (like the Camden resident Whitman), Williams and Ginsberg (who was born in Newark in 1926) have written in an idiom deeply American, in rhythms native to the land whose promise they have uneasily but energetically recognized.

There is yet another side of the man to be seen, the side in evidence in the San Francisco Be-In, or in the confrontation between the Hell's Angels and Berkeley peace marchers (gracefully resolved by Om-chanting Ginsberg), or during the chaos of Chicago (where he sang to protesters on the shore of Lake Michigan in the early morning hours, and he spoke of love to those about to meet the police).

He is now embarked on "A Poem of These States." Whitman began a long epic of the same name, worked on it with love for some 35 years, until his death. Ginsberg continues the verse into our time, writing now of Kansas, of California, of the war, of politicians, of young people, of that new consciousness he so beautifully sees in the heart of the coming American experience. With that vision, he is given, as he has put it, "a sense of being self-prophetic master of the universe."*

The poems come from *Howl and Other Poems* (1956) and *Planet News* (1968).

---

*"The Art of Poetry VIII: An Interview" (with Thomas Clark), *The Paris Review*, 37 (Spring 1966), 14-15. This was taken from a series of author interviews in which Allen Ginsberg was the eighth poet interviewed.

*"The Art of Poetry VIII," p. 55.

SUNFLOWER SUTRA[1]

I walked on the banks of the tincan banana dock and sat down under the huge shade of a Southern Pacific locomotive to look at the sunset over the box house hills and cry.
Jack Kerouac sat beside me on a busted rusty iron pole, companion, we thought the same thoughts of the soul, bleak and blue and sad-eyed, surrounded by the gnarled steel roots of trees of machinery.
The oily water on the river mirrored the red sky, sun sank on top of final Frisco peaks, no fish in that stream, no hermit in those mounts, just ourselves rheumy-eyed and hungover like old bums on the riverbank, tired and wily.
Look at the Sunflower, he said, there was a dead gray shadow against the sky, big as a man, sitting dry on top of a pile of ancient sawdust—
—I rushed up enchanted—it was my first sunflower, memories of Blake—my visions—Harlem
and Hells of the Eastern rivers, bridges clanking Joes Greasy Sandwiches, dead baby carriages, black treadless tires forgotten and unretreaded, the poem of the riverbank, condoms & pots, steel knives, nothing stainless, only the dank muck and the razor sharp artifacts passing into the past—
and the gray Sunflower poised against the sunset, crackly bleak and dusty with the smut and smog and smoke of olden locomotives in its eye—
corolla of bleary spikes pushed down and broken like a battered crown, seeds fallen out of its face, soon-to-be-toothless mouth of sunny air, sunrays obliterated on its hairy head like a dried wire spiderweb,
leaves stuck out like arms out of the stem, gestures from the sawdust root, broke pieces cf plaster fallen out of the black twigs, a dead fly in its ear,
Unholy battered old thing you were, my sunflower O my soul, I loved you then!
The grime was no man's grime but death and human locomotives,
all that dress of dust, that veil of darkened railroad skin, that smog of cheek, that eyelid of black mis'ry, that sooty hand or phallus or protuberance of artificial worse-than-dirt—industrial—modern—all that civilization spotting your crazy golden crown—
and those blear thoughts of death and dusty loveless eyes and ends and withered roots below, in the home-pile of sand and sawdust,

rubber dollar bills, skin of machinery, the guts and innards of the weeping coughing car, the empty lonely tincans with their rusty tongues alack, what more could I name, the smoked ashes of some cock cigar, the cunts of wheelbarrows and the milky breasts of cars, wornout asses out of chairs & sphincters of dynamos—all these
entangled in your mummied roots—and you there standing before me in the sunset, all your glory in your form!
A perfect beauty of a sunflower! a perfect excellent lovely sunflower existence! a sweet natural eye to the new hip moon, woke up alive and excited grasping in the sunset shadow sunrise golden monthly breeze!
How many flies buzzed round you innocent of your grime, while you cursed the heavens of the railroad and your flower soul?
Poor dead flower? when did you forget you were a flower? when did you look at your skin and decide you were an impotent dirty old locomotive? the ghost of a locomotive? the specter and shade of a once powerful mad American locomotive?
You were never no locomotive, Sunflower, you were a sunflower!
And you Locomotive, you are a locomotive, forget me not!
So I grabbed up the skeleton thick sunflower and stuck it at my side like a scepter,
and deliver my sermon to my soul, and Jack's soul too, and anyone who'll listen,
—We're not our skin of grime, we're not our dread bleak dusty imageless locomotive, we're all beautiful golden sunflowers inside, we're blessed by our own seed & golden hairy naked accomplishment-bodies growing into mad black formal sunflowers in the sunset, spied on by our eyes under the shadow of the mad locomotive riverbank sunset Frisco hilly tincan evening sitdown vision.

—Berkeley 1955

[1]*Sutra* a lecture; in Buddhism a sutra is a narrative that teaches some part of the life of the Buddha.

AMERICA

America I've given you all and now I'm nothing.
America two dollars and twentyseven cents January 17, 1956.
I can't stand my own mind.
America when will we end the human war?

Go fuck yourself with your atom bomb.
I don't feel good don't bother me.
I won't write my poem till I'm in my right mind.
America when will you be angelic?
When will you take off your clothes?
When will you look at yourself through the grave?
When will you be worthy of your million Trotskyites?
America why are your libraries full of tears?
America when will you send your eggs to India?
I'm sick of your insane demands.
When can I go into the supermarket and buy what I need with my good looks?
America after all it is you and I who are perfect not the next world.
Your machinery is too much for me.
You made me want to be a saint.
There must be some other way to settle this argument.
Burroughs[1] is in Tangiers I don't think he'll come back it's sinister.
Are you being sinister or is this some form of practical joke?
I'm trying to come to the point.
I refuse to give up my obsession.
America stop pushing I know what I'm doing.
America the plum blossoms are falling.
I haven't read the newspapers for months, everyday somebody goes on trial for murder.
America I feel sentimental about the Wobblies.[2]
America I used to be a communist when I was a kid I'm not sorry.
I smoke marijuana every chance I get.
I sit in my house for days on end and stare at the roses in the closet.
When I go to Chinatown I get drunk and never get laid.
My mind is made up there's going to be trouble.
You should have seen me reading Marx.
My psychoanalyst thinks I'm perfectly right.
I won't say the Lord's Prayer.
I have mystical visions and cosmic vibrations.
America I still haven't told you what you did to Uncle Max after he came over from Russia.

I'm addressing you.
Are you going to let your emotional life be run by Time Magazine?
I'm obsessed by Time Magazine.
I read it every week.
Its cover stares at me every time I slink past the corner candystore.
I read it in the basement of the Berkeley Public Library.

It's always telling me about responsibility. Businessmen are serious.
          Movie Producers are serious. Everybody's serious but me.
It occurs to me that I am America.
I am talking to myself again.

Asia is rising against me.
I haven't got a chinaman's chance.
I'd better consider my national resources.
My national resources consist of two joints of marijuana millions of
          genitals an unpublishable private literature that goes 1400
          miles an hour and twentyfive-thousand mental institutions.
I say nothing about my prisons nor the millions of underprivileged
          who live in my flowerpots under the light of five hundred
          suns.
I have abolished the whorehouses of France, Tangiers is the next
          to go.
My ambition is to be President despite the fact that I'm a Catholic.

America how can I write a holy litany in your silly mood?
I will continue like Henry Ford my strophes are as individual as
          his automobiles more so they're all different sexes.
America I will sell you strophes $2500 apiece $500 down on your
          old strophe
America free Tom Mooney[3]
America save the Spanish Loyalists
America Sacco & Vanzetti must not die
America I am the Scottsboro boys.[4]
America when I was seven momma took me to Communist Cell meetings
          they sold us garbanzos a handful per ticket a ticket costs a
          nickel and the speeches were free everybody was angelic and
          sentimental about the workers it was all so sincere you have
          no idea what a good thing the party was in 1935 Scott Nearing
          was a grand old man a real mensch Mother Bloor made me
          cry I once saw Israel Amter plain. Everybody must have been
          a spy.
America you don't really want to go to war.
America it's them bad Russians.
Them Russians them Russians and them Chinamen. And them Russians.
The Russia wants to eat us alive. The Russia's power mad. She wants
          to take our cars from out our garages.
Her wants to grab Chicago. Her needs a Red Readers' Digest. Her wants
          our auto plants in Siberia. Him big bureaucracy running our
          fillingstations.

That no good. Ugh. Him make Indians learn read. Him need big black
        niggers. Hah. Her make us all work sixteen hours a day. Help.
America this is quite serious.
America this is the impression I get from looking in the television set.
America is this correct?
I'd better get right down to the job.
It's true I don't want to join the Army or turn lathes in precision parts
        factories, I'm nearsighted and psychopathic anyway.
America I'm putting my queer shoulder to the wheel.

[1]*William Burroughs,* novelist and one-time drug addict. [2]*Wobblies,* members of the Industrial Workers of the World, a radical labor union. [3]*Tom Mooney* labor agitator (1883-1942) accused of throwing a bomb during an Armistice Day Parade in San Francisco in 1916. Charged with murder and sentenced to death, he was widely believed to be innocent. He was sentenced to life imprisonment, but was pardoned in 1939. [4]*Scottsboro boys* nine Negro boys accused of raping two white girls in Alabama. Five went to prison.

FIRST PARTY AT KEN KESEY'S[1] WITH HELL'S ANGELS

Cool black night thru the redwoods
cars parked outside in shade
behind the gate, stars dim above
the ravine, a fire burning by the side
porch and a few tired souls hunched over
in black leather jackets. In the huge
wooden house, a yellow chandelier
at 3AM the blast of loudspeakers
hi-fi Rolling Stones Ray Charles Beatles
Jumping Joe Jackson and twenty youths
dancing to the vibration thru the floor,
a little weed in the bathroom, girls in scarlet
tights, one muscular smooth skinned man
sweating dancing for hours, beer cans
bent littering the yard, a hanged man
sculpture dangling from a high creek branch,
children sleeping softly in bedroom bunks,
And 4 police cars parked outside the painted
gate, red lights revolving in the leaves.

                        December 1965

[1]*Ken Kesey* author of *One Flew Over the Cuckoo's Nest* and *Sometimes a Great Notion.* The party is described by journalist Tom Wolfe in *The Electric Kool-Aid Acid Test* (New York: Farrar Straus and Giroux, 1968; Bantam paperback, 1969).

from WICHITA VORTEX SUTRA

Is this the land that started war on China?
        This be the soil that thought Cold War for decades?
      Are these nervous naked trees & farmhouses
                             the vortex
                          of oriental anxiety molecules
      that've imagined   American Foreign Policy
             and magick'd up paranoia in Peking
                     and curtains of living blood
                             surrounding far Saigon?
Are these the towns where the language emerged
    from the mouths here
               that makes a Hell of riots in Dominica
     sustains the aging tyranny of Chiang in silent Taipeh city
     Paid for the lost French war in Algeria
          overthrew the Guatemalan polis in '54
     maintaining United Fruit's[1] banana greed
                          another thirteen years
         for the secret prestige of the Dulles family lawfirm?[2]

Here's Marysville—
     a black railroad engine in the children's park,
                       at rest—

and the Track Crossing
     with Cotton Belt flatcars
                 carrying autos west from Dallas
     Delaware & Hudson gondolas filled with power stuff—
    a line of boxcars far east as the eye can see
             carrying battle goods to cross the Rockies
          into the hands of rich longshoreman loading
                       ships on the Pacific—
     Oakland Army Terminal lights
               blue illumined all night now—
Crash of couplings and the great American train
          moves on carrying its cushioned load of metal doom
     Union Pacific linked together with your Hoosier Line
           followed by passive Wabash
                   rolling behind
         all Erie carrying cargo in the rear,
     Central Georgia's rust colored truck proclaiming
                   The Right Way, concluding
    the awesome poem writ by the train

                    across northern Kansas,
              land which gave right of way
              to the massing of metal meant for explosion
                                in Indochina—
Passing thru Waterville,
         Electronic machinery in the bus humming prophecy—
              paper signs blowing in cold wind,
                        mid-Sunday afternoon's silence
                                       in town
                   under frost-grey sky
                             that covers the horizon—
That the rest of earth is unseen,
                   an outer universe invisible,
                        Unknown except thru
                                  language
                                       airprint
                                            magic images

              or prophecy of the secret
                        heart the same
                        in Waterville as Saigon one human form:
                   When a woman's heart bursts in Waterville
                             a woman screams equal in Hanoi—
On to Wichita to prophesy! O frightful Bard!
         into the heart of the Vortex
                   where anxiety rings
                        the University with millionaire pressure,
              lonely crank telephone voices sighing in dread,
              and students waken trembling in their beds
                   with dreams of a new truth warm as meat,
                   little girls suspecting their elders of murder
                        committed by remote control machinery,
              boys with sexual bellies aroused
                        chilled in the heart by the mailman
              with a letter from an aging white haired General
                   Director of selection for service in
                                            Deathwar
                   all this black language
                             writ by machine!
                        O hopeless Fathers and Teachers
                        in Hué   do you know
                                  the same woe too?

         I'm an old man now, and a lonesome man in Kansas
                   but not afraid

     to speak my lonesomeness in a car,
     because not only my lonesomeness
       it's Ours, all over America,
           O tender fellows—
     & spoken lonesomeness is Prophecy
     in the moon 100 years ago or in
        the middle of Kansas now.
It's not the vast plains mute our mouths
       that fill at midnite with ecstatic language
    when our trembling bodies hold each other
       breast to breast on a mattress—
 Not the empty sky that hides
       the feeling from our faces
nor our skirts and trousers that conceal
    the bodylove emanating in a glow of beloved skin,
      white smooth abdomen down to the hair
        between our legs,
 It's not a God that bore us that forbid
    our Being, like a sunny rose
      all red with naked joy
    between our eyes & bellies, yes
All we do is for this frightened thing
    we call Love, want and lack—
  fear that we aren't the one whose body could be
    beloved of all the brides of Kansas City,
    kissed all over by every boy of Wichita—
   O but how many in their solitude weep aloud like me—
    On the bridge over Republican River
      almost in tears to know
        how to speak the right language—
   on the frosty broad road
      uphill between highway embankments
  I search for the language
    that is also yours—
almost all our language has been taxed by war.

               Spring 1966

---

  [1]*United Fruit Company,* founded in 1899, rapidly established itself as a monopoly in the banana trade in South America, where it has often played a role in Caribbean politics. [2]*The Dulles family* includes John Foster Dulles, U.S. Secretary of State (1953-1959) known for his favoring of "brinkmanship," that is, a doctrine of (a) instant retaliation by nuclear weapons in case of war and (b) threat of retaliation in case of serious challenge to U.S. interests. Allen Dulles, brother of John Foster, directed the Central Intelligence Agency (1953-1961).

WALES VISITATION

White fog lifting & falling on mountain-brow
        Trees moving in rivers of wind
                            The clouds arise
  as on a wave, gigantic eddy lifting mist
      above teeming ferns exquisitely swayed
                              along a green crag
      glimpsed thru mullioned glass in valley raine—

Bardic, O Self, Visitacione, tell naught
    but what seen by one man in a vale in Albion,
        of the folk, whose physical sciences end in Ecology,
                the wisdom of earthly relations,
    of mouths & eyes interknit ten centuries visible
        orchards of mind language manifest human,
  of the satanic thistle that raises its horned symmetry
    flowering above sister grass-daisies' pink tiny
                  bloomlets angelic as lightbulbs—

Remember 160 miles from London's symmetrical thorned tower
      & network of TV pictures flashing bearded your Self
    the lambs on the tree-nooked hillside this day bleating
    heard in Blake's old ear, & the silent thought of Wordsworth in
                            eld Stillness
  clouds passing through skeleton arches of Tintern Abbey—
      Bard Nameless as the Vast, babble to Vastness!

All the Valley quivered, one extended motion, wind
                  undulating on mossy hills

      a giant wash that sank white fog delicately down red runnels
                          on the mountainside
  whose leaf-branch tendrils moved asway
                  in granitic undertow down—
and lifted the floating Nebulous upward, and lifted the arms of the
                                          trees
      and lifted the grasses an instant in balance
          and lifted the lambs to hold still
  and lifted the green of the hill, in one solemn wave

A solid mass of Heaven, mist-infused, ebbs thru the vale,
    a wavelet of Immensity, lapping gigantic through Llanthony
                                    Valley,

   the length of all England, valley upon valley under Heaven's ocean
                                         tonned with cloud-hang,
         Heaven balanced on a grassblade—
Roar of the mountain wind slow, sigh of the body,
     One Being on the mountainside stirring gently
               Exquisite scales trembling everywhere in balance,
one motion thru the cloudy sky-floor shifting on the million
                                  feet of daisies,
one Majesty the motion that stirred wet grass quivering
     to the farthest tendril of white fog poured down
          through shivering flowers on the mountain's
                                      head—

No imperfection in the budded mountain,
    Valleys breathe, heaven and earth move together,
  daisies push inches of yellow air, vegetables tremble,
          green atoms shimmer in grassy mandalas,
sheep speckle the mountainside, revolving their jaws with empty
                                            eyes,
         horses dance in the warm rain,
  tree-lined canals network through live farmland,
         blueberries fringe stone walls
    on hill breasts nippled with hawthorn,
pheasants croak up meadow-bellies haired with fern—

Out, out on the hillside, into the ocean sound, into delicate
                                  gusts of wet air,
Fall on the ground, O great Wetness, O Mother, No harm on
                                      thy body!
Stare close, no imperfection in the grass,
          each flower Buddha-eye, repeating the story,
                the myriad-formed soul
Kneel before the foxglove raising green buds, mauve bells drooped
    doubled down the stem trembling antennae,
  & look in the eyes of the branded lambs that stare
    breathing stockstill under dripping hawthorn—
I lay down mixing my beard with the wet hair of the mountainside,
    smelling the brown vagina-moist ground, harmless,
       tasting the violet thistle-hair, sweetness—
One being so balanced, so vast, that its softest breath
    moves every floweret in the stillness on the valley floor,
  trembles lamb-hair hung gossamer rain-beaded in the grass,
lifts trees on their roots, birds in the great draught
     hiding their strength in the rain, bearing same weight,

Groan thru breast and neck, a great Oh! to earth heart
                            Calling our Presence together
          The great secret is no secret
                Senses fit the winds,
                        Visible is visible,
rain-mist curtains wave through the bearded vale,
                grey atoms wet the wind's Kaballah

Crosslegged on a rock in dusk rain,
            rubber booted in soft grass, mind moveless,
breath trembles in white daisies by the roadside,
                Heaven breath and my own symmetric
      Airs wavering thru antlered green fern
drawn in my navel, same breath as breathes thru Capel-Y-Ffn,
            Sounds of Aleph and Aum
                    through forests of gristle,
      my skull and Lord Hereford's Knob equal,
                          All Albion one.

What did I notice? Particulars! The
            vision of the great One is myriad—
smoke curls upward from ash tray,
            house fire burned low,
The night, still wet & moody black heaven
                    starless
upward in motion with wet wind.

                          July 29, 1967 (LSD)—August 3, 1967 (London)

FRANK O'HARA

Frank O'Hara (1926, Baltimore, Maryland—1966, New York City) was a playwright of the off-Broadway theatre in New York City and the Poet's Theatre of Cambridge, Massachusetts. He also worked as a curator for the Museum of Modern Art in New York City and was a contributor of articles to *Art News* magazine. He attended Harvard and the University of Michigan. "Steps" is from *Lunch Poems* (1964).

STEPS

How funny you are today New York
like Ginger Rogers in *Swingtime*
and St. Bridget's steeple leaning a little to the left

here I have just jumped out of a bed full of V-days
(I got tired of D-days) and blue you there still
accepts me foolish and free
all I want is a room up there
and you in it
and even the traffic halt so thick is a way
for people to rub up against each other
and when their surgical appliances lock
they stay together
for the rest of the day (what a day)
I go by to check a slide and I say
that painting's not so blue

where's Lana Turner
she's out eating
and Garbo's backstage at the Met
everyone's taking their coat off
so they can show a rib-cage to the rib-watchers
and the park's full of dancers and their tights and shoes
in little bags
who are often mistaken for worker-outers at the West Side Y
why not
the Pittsburgh Pirates shout because they won
and in a sense we're all winning
we're alive

the apartment was vacated by a gay couple
who moved to the country for fun
they moved a day too soon
even the stabbings are helping the population explosion
though in the wrong country
and all those liars have left the UN
the Seagram Building's no longer rivalled in interest
not that we need liquor (we just like it)

and the little box is out on the sidewalk
next to the delicatessen
so the old man can sit on it and drink beer
and get knocked off it by his wife later in the day
while the sun is still shining

oh god it's wonderful
to get out of bed
and drink too much coffee
and smoke too many cigarettes
and love you so much

1961

ROBERT CREELEY

Charles Olson dedicated *The Maximus Poems* to Robert Creeley, calling him "the Figure of Outward." Creeley was Olson's student at Black Mountain College and editor of *The Black Mountain Review*. Creeley was born in 1926 in Arlington, Massachusetts. He went to school at Harvard, Black Mountain College (North Carolina), and the University of New Mexico, and he has taught in many schools, among them the University of New Mexico and the New York State University, Buffalo. He worked with the American Field Service in India and Burma. He is the author of a novel, *The Island*. He now lives in Bolinas, California. The poems come from *If You* (1956), *For Love* (1962), and *Words* (1967).

IF YOU

If you were going to get a pet
what kind of animal would you get.

A soft bodied dog, a hen—
feathers and fur to begin it again.

When the sun goes down and it gets dark
I saw an animal in a park.

Bring it home, to give it to you.
I have seen animals break in two.

You were hoping for something soft
and loyal and clean and wondrously careful—

a form of otherwise vicious habit
can have long ears and be called a rabbit.

Dead. Died. Will die. Want.
Morning, midnight. I asked you

if you were going to get a pet
what kind of animal would you get.

OH NO

If you wander far enough
you will come to it
and when you get there
they will give you a place to sit

for yourself only, in a nice chair,
and all your friends will be there
with smiles on their faces
and they will likewise all have places.

THE RHYTHM

It is all a rhythm,
from the shutting
door, to the window
opening,

the seasons, the sun's
light, the moon,
the oceans, the
growing of things,

the mind in men
personal, recurring
in them again,
thinking the end

is not the end, the
time returning,
themselves dead but
someone else coming.

If in death I am dead,
then in life also
dying, dying . . .
And the women cry and die.

The little children
grow only to old men.
The grass dries,
the force goes.

I KNOW A MAN

As I sd to my
friend, because I am
always talking,—John, I

sd, which was not his
name, the darkness sur-
rounds us, what

can we do against
it, or else, shall we &
why not, buy a goddamn big car,

drive, he sd, for
christ's sake, look
out where yr going.

ANGER

1

The time is.
The air seems a cover,
the room is quiet.

She moves, she
had moved. He
heard her.

The children
sleep, the dog fed,
the house around them

is open, descriptive,
a truck through the walls,
lights bright there,

glaring, the sudden
roar of its motor, all
familiar impact

as it passed
so close. He
hated it.

But what does she answer.
She moves
away from it.

In all they save,
in the way of his saving
the clutter, the accumulation

of the expected disorder—
as if each dirtiness,
each blot, blurred

happily, gave
purpose, happily—
she is not enough there.

He is angry. His
face grows—as if
a moon rose

of black light,
convulsively darkening,
as if life were black.

It is black.
It is an open
hole of horror, of

nothing as if not
enough there is
nothing. A pit—

which he recognizes,
familiar, sees
the use in, a hole

for anger and
fills it
with himself,

yet watches on
the edge of it,
as if she were

not to be pulled in,
a hand could
stop him. Then

as the shouting
grows and grows
louder and louder

with spaces
of the same open
silence, the darkness,

in and out, him-
self between them,
stands empty and

holding out his
hands to both,
now screaming

it cannot be
the same, she
waits in the one

while the other
moans in the hole
in the floor, in the wall. . . .

2

Is there some odor
which is anger,

a face
which is rage.

I think I think
but find myself in it.

The pattern
is only resemblance.

I cannot see myself
but as what I see, an

object but a man,
with lust for forgiveness,

raging, from that vantage,
secure in the purpose,

double, split.
Is it merely intention,

a sign quickly adapted,
shifted to make

a horrible place
for self-satisfaction.

I rage.
I rage, I rage.

3

You did it,
and didn't want to,

and it was simple.
You were not involved,

even if your head was cut off,
or each finger

twisted
from its shape until it broke,

and you screamed too
with the other, in pleasure.

4

Face me,
in the dark,
my face. See me.

It is the cry
I hear all
my life, my own

voice, my
eye locked in
self sight, not

the world what
ever it is
but the close

breathing beside
me I reach out
for, feel as

warmth in
my hands then
returned. The rage

is what I
want, what
I cannot give

to myself, of
myself, in
the world.

5

After, what
is it—as if
the sun had

been wrong to return,
again. It was
another life, a

day, some
time gone, it
was done.

But also
the pleasure, the
opening

relief
even in what
was so hated.

6

All you say you want
to do to yourself you do
to someone else as yourself

and we sit between you
waiting for whatever will
be at last the real end of you.

ROBERT BLY

Robert Bly (born 1926, Madison, Minnesota, attended Harvard and the University of Iowa) is a translator of poetry and a publisher as well as a poet. His press is The Seventies Press, and the magazine he edits is called *The Seventies* (both were formerly called *The Sixties*). He has translated European and South American poetry. He founded American Writers Against the Vietnam War with David Ray (1966) and so helped to organize a series of readings to oppose the war. In 1968 he won the National Book Award in poetry. The poems are from *Silence in the Snowy Fields* (1962), *The Light Around the Body* (1967), *Twenty Poems of Pablo Neruda* (translated in collaboration with James Wright, 1967), and *The Teeth-Mother Naked at Last* (1970).

DRIVING TOWARD THE LAC QUI PARLE RIVER

I

I am driving; it is dusk; Minnesota.
The stubble field catches the last growth of sun.
The soybeans are breathing on all sides.
Old men are sitting before their houses on carseats
In the small towns. I am happy,
The moon rising above the turkey sheds.

II

The small world of the car
Plunges through the deep fields of the night,
On the road from Willmar to Milan.
This solitude covered with iron
Moves through the fields of night
Penetrated by the noise of crickets.

III

Nearly to Milan, suddenly a small bridge,
And water kneeling in the moonlight.
In small towns the houses are built right on the ground;
The lamplight falls on all fours in the grass.
When I reach the river, the full moon covers it;
A few people are talking low in a boat.

ODE TO MY SOCKS[1]

Maru Mori brought me
a pair
of socks
which she knitted herself
with her sheep-herder's hands,
two socks as soft
as rabbits.
I slipped my feet
into them
as though into
two
cases
knitted
with threads of
twilight
and goatskin.
Violent socks,
my feet were
two fish made
of wool,
two long sharks
seablue, shot
through
by one golden thread,
two immense blackbirds,
two cannons,
my feet
were honored
in this way
by
these

heavenly
socks.
They were
so handsome
for the first time
my feet seemed to me
unacceptable
like two decrepit
firemen, firemen
unworthy
of that woven
fire,
of those glowing
socks.

Nevertheless
I resisted
the sharp temptation
to save them somewhere
as schoolboys
keep
fireflies,
as learned men
collect
sacred texts,
I resisted
the mad impulse
to put them
in a golden
cage
and each day give them
birdseed
and pieces of pink melon.
Like explorers
in the jungle who hand
over the very rare
green deer
to the spit
and eat it
with remorse,
I stretched out
my feet
and pulled on

the magnificent
socks
and then my shoes.

The moral
of my ode is this:
beauty is twice
beauty
and what is good is doubly
good
when it is a matter of two socks
made of wool
in winter.

—*by Pablo Neruda*

[1]*Ode to My Socks* a translation of the poem "Oda a mis calcetines" by the contemporary Chilean poet Pablo Neruda.

LOOKING INTO A FACE

Conversation brings us so close! Opening
The surfs of the body,
Bringing fish up near the sun,
And stiffening the backbones of the sea!

I have wandered in a face, for hours,
Passing through dark fires.
I have risen to a body
Not yet born,
Existing like a light around the body,
Through which the body moves like a sliding moon.

COME WITH ME

Come with me into those things that have felt this despair for so long—
Those removed Chevrolet wheels that howl with a terrible loneliness,
Lying on their backs in the cindery dirt, like men drunk, and naked,
Staggering off down a hill at night to drown at last in the pond.
Those shredded inner tubes abandoned on the shoulders of thruways,
Black and collapsed bodies, that tried and burst,

And were left behind;
And the curly steel shavings, scattered about on garage benches,
Sometimes still warm, gritty when we hold them,
Who have given up, and blame everything on the government,
And those roads in South Dakota that feel around in the darkness . . .

HATRED OF MEN WITH BLACK HAIR

I hear voices praising Tshombe, and the Portuguese
In Angola, these are the men who skinned Little Crow!
We are all their sons, skulking
In back rooms, selling nails with trembling hands!

We distrust every person on earth with black hair;
We send teams to overthrow Chief Joseph's government;
We train natives to kill Presidents with blowdarts;
We have men loosening the nails on Noah's ark.

The State Department floats in the heavy jellies near the bottom
Like exhausted crustaceans, like squids who are confused,
Sending out beams of black light to the open sea,
Fighting their fraternal feeling for the great landlords.

We have violet rays that light up the jungles at night, showing
The friendly populations; we are teaching the children of ritual
To overcome their longing for life, and we send
Sparks of black light that fit the holes in the generals' eyes.

Underneath all the cement of the Pentagon
There is a drop of Indian blood preserved in snow:
Preserved from a trail of blood that once led away
From the stockade, over the snow, the trail now lost.

COUNTING SMALL-BONED BODIES

Let's count the bodies over again.

If we could only make the bodies smaller,
The size of skulls,
We could make a whole plain white with skulls in the moonlight!

If we could only make the bodies smaller,
Maybe we could get
A whole year's kill in front of us on a desk!

If we could only make the bodies smaller,
We could fit
A body into a finger-ring, for a keepsake forever.

SLEET STORM ON THE MERRITT PARKWAY

I look out at the white sleet covering the still streets
As we drive through Scarsdale—
The sleet began falling as we left Connecticut,
And the winter leaves swirled in the wet air after cars
Like hands suddenly turned over in a conversation.
Now the frost has nearly buried the short grass of March.
Seeing the sheets of sleet untouched on the wide streets,
I think of the many comfortable homes stretching for miles,
Two and three stories, solid, with polished floors,
With white curtains in the upstairs bedrooms,
And small perfume flagons of black glass on the window sills,
And warm bathrooms with guest towels, and electric lights—
What a magnificent place for a child to grow up!
And yet the children end in the river of price-fixing,
Or in the snowy field of the insane asylum.
The sleet falls—so many cars moving toward New York—
Last night we argued about the Marines invading Guatemala in 1947,
The United Fruit Company had one water spigot for 200 families,
And the ideals of America, our freedom to criticize,
The slave systems of Rome and Greece, and no one agreed.

from THE TEETH-MOTHER NAKED AT LAST

II

Excellent Roman knives slip along the ribs.

A stronger man starts to jerk up the strips of flesh.

Let's hear it again, you believe in the Father, the Son, and the Holy Ghost?

A long scream unrolls.

More.

From the political point of view, democratic institutions are being built in Vietnam, wouldn't you agree?

A green parrot shudders under the fingernails.
Blood jumps in the pocket.
The scream lashes like a tail.

"Let us not be deterred from our task by the voices of dissent. . . ."

The whines of jets
pierce like a long needle.

As soon as the President finishes his press conference, black wings carry off the words,
bits of flesh still clinging to them.

*   *   *

The ministers lie, the professors lie, the television lies, the priests lie. . . .
These lies mean that the country wants to die.
Lie after lie starts out into the prairie grass,
like enormous trains of Conestoga wagons. . . .

And a long desire for death flows out, guiding
the enormous caravans from beneath,
stringing together the vague and foolish words.

It is a desire to eat death,
to gobble it down,
to rush on it like a cobra with mouth open,

It's a desire to take death inside,
to feel it burning inside, pushing out velvety hairs,
like a clothes brush in the intestines

This is the thrill that leads the President on to lie

*   *   *

The Chief Executive enters; the Press Conference begins:
First the President lies about the date the Appalachian Mountains rose

Then he lies about the population of Chicago, then about the weight of the adult eagle, next about the acreage of the Everglades

He lies about the number of fish taken every year in the Arctic, he has private information about which city *is* the capital of Wyoming, he lies about the birthplace of Attila the Hun

He lies about the composition of the amniotic fluid, he insists that Luther was never a German, and insists that only the Protestants sold indulgences,
That Pope Leo X *wanted* to reform the church, but the "liberal elements" prevented him,

That the Peasants' War was fomented by Italians from the North.
And the Attorney General lies about the time the sun sets.

*   *   *

This is only the deep longing for death.
It is the longing for someone to come and take us by the hand to where they all are sleeping:
where the Egyptian Pharoahs are asleep, and your own mother,
and all those disappeared children, who used to go around with you in a swing at grade school. . . .
Do not be angry at the President—he is longing to take in his hand the locks of death hair—
to meet his own children sleeping, or unborn. . . .
He is drifting sideways toward the dusty places

VI

But if one of those children came near that we have set on fire,
came toward you like a gray barn, walking,
you would howl like a wind tunnel in a hurricane,
you would tear at your shirt with blue hands,
you would drive over your own child's wagon trying to back up,
the pupils of your eyes would go wild—

If a child came by burning, you would dance on a lawn,
trying to walk into the air, digging into your cheeks,
you would ram your head against the wall of your bedroom
like a bull penned too long in his moody pen—

If one of those children came toward me with both hands
in the air, fire rising along both elbows,
I would suddenly go back to my animal brain,
I would drop on all fours, screaming,
my vocal chords would turn blue, yours would too,
it would be two days before I could play with my own children again.

JAMES WRIGHT

James Wright was born in 1927 in Martin's Ferry, Ohio. He went to school at Kenyon College and the University of Washington, and he is now a member of the English department of Hunter College of the City University of New York. He has also taught at the University of Minnesota and at Macalester College (St. Paul, Minnesota). He translates prose and poetry from German, French, and Spanish. In collaboration with Robert Bly he has translated poems by the Chilean poet Pablo Neruda. He lives in New York City. The poems come from *The Branch Will Not Break* (1963).

A BLESSING

Just off the highway to Rochester, Minnesota,
Twilight bounds softly forth on the grass.
And the eyes of those two Indian ponies
Darken with kindness.
They have come gladly out of the willows
To welcome my friend and me.
We step over the barbed wire into the pasture
Where they have been grazing all day, alone.
They ripple tensely, they can hardly contain their happiness
That we have come.
They bow shyly as wet swans. They love each other.
There is no loneliness like theirs.
At home once more,
They begin munching the young tufts of spring in the darkness.
I would like to hold the slenderer one in my arms,
For she has walked over to me
And nuzzled my left hand.
She is black and white,
Her mane falls wild on her forehead,
And the light breeze moves me to caress her long ear
That is delicate as the skin over a girl's wrist.
Suddenly I realize
That if I stepped out of my body I would break
Into blossom.

AUTUMN BEGINS IN MARTINS FERRY, OHIO

In the Shreve High football stadium,
I think of Polacks nursing long beers in Tiltonsville,
And gray faces of Negroes in the blast furnace at Benwood,
And the ruptured night watchman of Wheeling Steel,
Dreaming of heroes.

All the proud fathers are ashamed to go home.
Their women cluck like starved pullets,
Dying for love.

Therefore,
Their sons grow suicidally beautiful
At the beginning of October,
And gallop terribly against each other's bodies.

STAGES ON A JOURNEY WESTWARD

1

I began in Ohio.
I still dream of home.
Near Mansfield, enormous dobbins enter dark barns in autumn,
Where they can be lazy, where they can munch little apples,
Or sleep long.
But by night now, in the bread lines my father
Prowls, I cannot find him: So far off,
1500 miles or so away, and yet
I can hardly sleep.
In a blue rag the old man limps to my bed,
Leading a blind horse
Of gentleness.
In 1932, grimy with machinery, he sang me
A lullaby of a goosegirl.
Outside the house, the slag heaps waited.

2

In western Minnesota, just now,
I slept again.
In my dream, I crouched over a fire.

The only human beings between me and the Pacific Ocean
Were old Indians, who wanted to kill me.
They squat and stare for hours into small fires
Far off in the mountains.
The blades of their hatchets are dirty with the grease
Of huge, silent buffaloes.

3

It is dawn.
I am shivering,
Even beneath a huge eiderdown.
I came in last night, drunk,
And left the oil stove cold.
I listen a long time, now, to the flurries.
Snow howls all around me, out of the abandoned prairies.
It sounds like the voices of bums and gamblers,
Rattling through the bare nineteenth-century whorehouses
In Nevada.

4

Defeated for re-election,
The half-educated sheriff of Mukilteo, Washington,
Has been drinking again.
He leads me up the cliff, tottering.
Both drunk, we stand among the graves.
Miners paused here on the way up to Alaska.
Angry, they spaded their broken women's bodies
Into ditches of crab grass.
I lie down between tombstones.
At the bottom of the cliff
America is over and done with.
America,
Plunged into the dark furrows
Of the sea again.

W. S. MERWIN

W. S. Merwin has written plays for The Poets' Theatre in Cambridge, Massachusetts. He is a translator of two long narrative poems, *The Song of Roland* (from medieval French) and *The Cid* (from medieval Spanish). He was born in New York City in 1927, went to Princeton, and now lives in this country, although for many years he lived abroad, in England, France, Majorca, and Portugal. The poems come from *The Moving Target* (1963) and *The Lice* (1967).

AIR

Naturally it is night.
Under the overturned lute with its
One string I am going my way
Which has a strange sound.

This way the dust, that way the dust.
I listen to both sides
But I keep right on.
I remember the leaves sitting in judgment
And then winter.

I remember the rain with its bundle of roads.
The rain taking all its roads.
Nowhere.

Young as I am, old as I am,

I forget tomorrow, the blind man.
I forget the life among the buried windows.
The eyes in the curtains.
The wall
Growing through the immortelles.
I forget silence
The owner of the smile.

This must be what I wanted to be doing,
Walking at night between the two deserts,
Singing.

IN ONE OF THE RETREATS OF MORNING

There are still bits of night like closed eyes in the walls
And at their feet the large brotherhood of broken stones
Is still asleep

I go quietly along the edge of their garden
Looking at the few things they grow for themselves

ANNE SEXTON

Anne Sexton has been a student of Robert Lowell and a friend of Sylvia Plath, whom she met in Lowell's seminar at Boston University. She was born in 1928 in Newton, Massachusetts, attended Garland Junior College and the Radcliffe Institute for Independent Study, and now lives in Weston, Massachusetts, with her husband and her two daughters. The poems come from *To Bedlam and Part Way Back* (1960) and *Live or Die* (1966).

UNKNOWN GIRL IN THE MATERNITY WARD

Child, the current of your breath is six days long.
You lie, a small knuckle on my white bed;
lie, fisted like a snail, so small and strong
at my breast. Your lips are animals; you are fed
with love. At first hunger is not wrong.
The nurses nod their caps; you are shepherded
down starch halls with the other unnested throng
in wheeling baskets. You tip like a cup; your head
moving to my touch. You sense the way we belong.
But this is an institution bed.
You will not know me very long.

The doctors are enamel. They want to know
the facts. They guess about the man who left me,
some pendulum soul, going the way men go
and leave you full of child. But our case history
stays blank. All I did was let you grow.
Now we are here for all the ward to see.
They thought I was strange, although
I never spoke a word. I burst empty
of you, letting you learn how the air is so.
The doctors chart the riddle they ask of me
and I turn my head away. I do not know.

Yours is the only face I recognize.
Bone at my bone, you drink my answers in.
Six times a day I prize
your need, the animals of your lips, your skin
growing warm and plump. I see your eyes
lifting their tents. They are blue stones, they begin
to outgrow their moss. You blink in surprise
and I wonder what you can see, my funny kin,
as you trouble my silence. I am a shelter of lies.
Should I learn to speak again, or hopeless in
such sanity will I touch some face I recognize?

Down the hall the baskets start back. My arms
fit you like a sleeve, they hold
catkins of your willows, the wild bee farms
of your nerves, each muscle and fold
of your first days. Your old man's face disarms
the nurses. But the doctors return to scold
me. I speak. It is you my silence harms.
I should have known; I should have told
them something to write down. My voice alarms
my throat. "Name of father—none." I hold
you and name you bastard in my arms.

And now that's that. There is nothing more
that I can say or lose.
Others have traded life before
and could not speak. I tighten to refuse
your owling eyes, my fragile visitor.
I touch your cheeks, like flowers. You bruise
against me. We unlearn. I am a shore
rocking you off. You break from me. I choose
your only way, my small inheritor
and hand you off, trembling the selves we lose.
Go child, who is my sin and nothing more.

CONSORTING WITH ANGELS

I was tired of being a woman,
tired of the spoons and the pots,

tired of my mouth and my breasts,
tired of the cosmetics and the silks.
There were still men who sat at my table,
circled around the bowl I offered up.
The bowl was filled with purple grapes
and the flies hovered in for the scent
and even my father came with his white bone.
But I was tired of the gender of things.

Last night I had a dream
and I said to it . . .
"You are the answer.
You will outlive my husband and my father."
In that dream there was a city made of chains
where Joan was put to death in man's clothes
and the nature of the angels went unexplained,
no two made in the same species,
one with a nose, one with an ear in its hand,
one chewing a star and recording its orbit,
each one like a poem obeying itself,
performing God's functions,
a people apart.

"You are the answer,"
I said, and entered,
lying down on the gates of the city.
Then the chains were fastened around me
and I lost my common gender and my final aspect.
Adam was on the left of me
and Eve was on the right of me,
both thoroughly inconsistent with the world of reason.
We wove our arms together
and rode under the sun.
I was not a woman anymore,
not one thing or the other.

O daughters of Jerusalem,
the king has brought me into his chamber.
I am black and I am beautiful.
I've been opened and undressed.

I have no arms or legs.
I'm all one skin like a fish.
I'm no more a woman
than Christ was a man.

February 1963

LIVE

Live or die, but don't poison everything . . .

Well, death's been here
for a long time—
it has a hell of a lot
to do with hell
and suspicion of the eye
and the religious objects
and how I mourned them
when they were made obscene
by my dwarf-heart's doodle.
The chief ingredient
is mutilation.
And mud, day after day,
mud like a ritual,
and the baby on the platter,
cooked but still human,
cooked also with little maggots,
sewn onto it maybe by somebody's mother,
the damn bitch!

Even so,
I kept right on going on,
a sort of human statement,
lugging myself as if
I were a sawed-off body
in the trunk, the steamer trunk.
This became a perjury of the soul.
It became an outright lie
and even though I dressed the body
it was still naked, still killed.

It was caught
in the first place at birth,
like a fish.
But I played it, dressed it up,
dressed it up like somebody's doll.
Is life something you play?
And all the time wanting to get rid of it?
And further, everyone yelling at you
to shut up. And no wonder!
People don't like to be told
that you're sick
and then be forced
to watch
you
come
down with the hammer.

Today life opened inside me like an egg
and there inside
after considerable digging
I found the answer.
What a bargain!
There was the sun
her yolk moving feverishly,
tumbling her prize—
and you realize that she does this daily!
I'd known she was a purifier
but I hadn't thought
she was solid,
hadn't known she was an answer.
God! It's a dream,
lovers sprouting in the yard
like celery stalks
and better,
a husband straight as a redwood,
two daughters, two sea urchins,
picking roses off my hackles.
If I'm on fire they dance around it
and cook marshmallows.
And if I'm ice
they simply skate on me
in little ballet costumes.

Here,
all along,
thinking I was a killer,
anointing myself daily
with my little poisons.
But no.
I'm an empress.
I wear an apron.
My typewriter writes.
It didn't break the way it warned.
Even crazy, I'm as nice
as a chocolate bar.
Even with the witches' gymnastics
they trust my incalculable city,
my corruptible bed.

O dearest three,
I make a soft reply.
The witch comes on
and you paint her pink.
I come with kisses in my hood
and the sun, the smart one,
rolling in my arms.
So I say *Live*
and turn my shadow three times round
to feed our puppies as they come,
the eight Dalmatians we didn't drown,
despite the warnings: The abort! The destroy!
Despite the pails of water that waited
to drown them, to pull them down like stones,
they came, each one headfirst,
blowing bubbles the color of cataract-blue
and fumbling for the tiny tits.
Just last week, eight Dalmatians,
¾ of a lb., lined up like cord wood
each
like a
birch tree.
I promise to love more if they come,
because in spite of cruelty
and the stuffed railroad cars for the ovens,
I am not what I expected. Not an Eichmann.

The poison just didn't take.
So I won't hang around in my hospital shift,
repeating The Black Mass and all of it.
I say *Live, Live* because of the sun,
the dream, the excitable gift.

February the last, 1966

JONATHAN WILLIAMS

Jonathan Williams was born in Asheville, North Carolina, in 1929. He has attended Princeton, the Institute of Design (Chicago), Atelier 17, (New York City), and Black Mountain College (North Carolina). He is represented here by his "found-object" poems, poems he discovered rather than invented. Williams lives in Highlands, North Carolina, or at Corn Close, Dentdale, Sedbergh, Yorkshire, England. The poems come from *An Ear in Bartram's Tree* (1969).

FROM UNCLE JAKE CARPENTER'S ANTHOLOGY OF DEATH ON THREE-MILE CREEK

Loney Ollis
age 84
dide jun 10 1871

grates dere honter
wreked bee trees for hony
cild ratell snak by 100
cild dere by thousen

i nod him well

THE EPITAPH ON UNCLE NICK GRINDSTAFF'S GRAVE ON THE IRON MOUNTAIN ABOVE SHADY VALLEY, TENNESSEE

LIVED ALONE   SUFFERED ALONE   DIED ALONE

PAINT SIGN ON A ROUGH ROCK YONSIDE OF BOONE SIDE OF SHADY VALLEY

BEPREPA
REDTO
MEETGO
D

ADRIENNE RICH

Adrienne Rich was born in Baltimore, Maryland, in 1929. She attended Radcliffe College. She has lectured in English or writing at several colleges and universities. Her work as a translator of Dutch poetry has attracted the sponsorship of the Bollingen Foundation. A widow since 1971, she has three sons. She lives in New York City. The poem comes from *Necessities of Life* (1966), a finalist in the National Book Award competition of that year.

AFTER DARK

I

You are falling asleep and I sit looking at you
old tree of life
old man whose death I wanted
I can't stir you up now.

Faintly a phonograph needle
whirs round in the last groove
eating my heart to dust.
That terrible record! how it played

down years, wherever I was
in foreign languages even
over and over, *I know you better*
than you know yourself   I know

you better than you know
yourself   I know
you   until, self-maimed,
I limped off, torn at the roots,

stopped singing a whole year,
got a new body, new breath,
got children, croaked for words,
forgot to listen

or read your *mene tekel* fading on the wall,
woke up one morning
and knew myself your daughter.
Blood is a sacred poison.

Now, unasked, you give ground.
We only want to stifle
what's stifling us already.
Alive now, root to crown, I'd give

—oh,—something—not to know
our struggles now are ended.
I seem to hold you, cupped
in my hands, and disappearing.

When your memory fails—
no more to scourge my inconsistencies—
the sashcords of the world fly loose.
A window crashes

suddenly down. I go to the woodbox
and take a stick of kindling
to prop the sash again.
I grow protective toward the world.

II

Now let's away from prison—
Underground seizures!
I used to huddle in the grave
I'd dug for you and bite

my tongue for fear it would babble
—Darling—
I thought they'd find me there
someday, sitting upright, shrunken,

my hair like roots and in my lap
a mess of broken pottery—
wasted libation—
and you embalmed beside me.

No, let's away. Even now
there's a walk between doomed elms
(whose like we shall not see much longer)
and something—grass and water—

an old dream-photograph.
I'll sit with you there and tease you
for wisdom, if you like,
waiting till the blunt barge

bumps along the shore.
Poppies burn in the twilight
like smudge pots.
I think you hardly see me

but—this is the dream now—
your fears blow out,
off, over the water.
At the last, your hand feels steady.

GREGORY CORSO

Gregory Corso (1930, New York City) grew up in an orphanage and in boys' homes. He dedicated his second book of poems *(Gasoline)* to "the angels of Clinton Prison who, in my 17th year, handed me, from all the cells surrounding me, books of illumination." He has worked as a manual laborer, a newspaper reporter, and a merchant seaman, and has traveled widely. During the fifties he became friends with Jack Kerouac and Allen Ginsberg. The poems are from *Gasoline* (1958), *The Happy Birthday of Death* (1960), and *Long Live Man* (1962).

LAST NIGHT I DROVE A CAR

Last night I drove a car
    not knowing how to drive
    not owning a car
I drove and knocked down
    people I loved
    . . . went 120 through one town.

I stopped at Hedgeville
    and slept in the back seat
    . . . excited about my new life.

SUN

(Automatic Poem)

Sun hypnotic! holy ball protracted long and sure! firey goblet! day-babble!
Sun, sun-webbed heat! tropic goblet dry! spider thirst! Sun, unwater!
Sun misery sun ire sun sick sun dead sun rot sun relic!
Sun o'er Afric sky low and tipped, spilt, almost empty, hollow vial,
    sunbone, sunstone, iron sun, sundial.
Sun dinosaur of electric motion extinct and fossiled, babble on!
Sun, season of the seasun, catching actual sunfish, on the green shore
    sunbathing like a madness.

Sun eros hellish superreal conglomeration of miasmatic ire!
Sun, sun-downed beings in desert life astounded, go down!
Sun circus! tent of helion, apollo, rha, sol, sun, exhult!
The sun like a blazing ship went down in Teliphicci lake.
The sun like a blazing disc of jelly slid over the Teliphiccian alps.
The sun leads the night and follows the night and leads the night.
The sun can be chariot-driven.
The sun like a blazing lollipop can be sucked.
The sun is shaped like a curved beckoning finger.
The sun spins walks dances skips runs.
The sun favors palm citrics tubercular-lungs
The sun eats up Teliphicci lake and alps every rising.
The sun does not know what it is to like or dislike.
The sun all my life went down in Teliphicci lake.
O constant hole where all beyond is true Byzantium.

FRIEND

Friends be kept
Friends be gained
And even friends lost be friends regained
He had no foes he made them all into *friends*
A friend will die for you
Acquaintances can never make friends
Some friends want to be everybody's friend
There are friends who take you away from friends
Friends believe in friendship with a vengeance!
Some friends always want to do you favors
Some always want to get NEAR you
You can't do this to me I'm your FRIEND
My friends said FDR
Let's be friends says the USSR
Old Scrooge knew a joy in a friendless Christmas
Leopold and Loeb planning in the night!
Et tu Brute
I have many friends yet sometimes I am nobody's friend
The majority of friends are male
Girls always prefer male friends
Friends know when you're troubled
It's what they crave for!
The bonds of friendship are not inseparable
Those who haven't any friends and want some are often creepy

Those who have friends and don't want them are doomed
Those who haven't any friends and don't want any are grand
Those who have friends and want them seem sadly human
Sometimes I scream Friends are bondage! A madness!
All a waste of INDIVIDUAL *time*—
Without friends life would be different not miserable
Does one need a friend in heaven—

MARRIAGE

Should I get married? Should I be good?
Astound the girl next door with my velvet suit and faustus hood?
Don't take her to movies but to cemeteries
tell all about werewolf bathtubs and forked clarinets
then desire her and kiss her and all the preliminaries
and she going just so far and I understanding why
not getting angry saying You must feel! It's beautiful to feel!
Instead take her in my arms lean against an old crooked tombstone
and woo her the entire night the constellations in the sky—

When she introduces me to her parents
back straightened, hair finally combed, strangled by a tie,
should I sit knees together on their 3rd degree sofa
and not ask Where's the bathroom?
How else to feel other than I am,
often thinking Flash Gordon soap—
O how terrible it must be for a young man
seated before a family and the family thinking
We never saw him before! He wants our Mary Lou!
After tea and homemade cookies they ask What do you do for a living?
Should I tell them? Would they like me then?
Say All right get married, we're losing a daughter
but we're gaining a son—
And should I then ask Where's the bathroom?

O God, and the wedding! All her family and her friends
and only a handful of mine all scroungy and bearded
just wait to get at the drinks and food—
And the priest! he looking at me as if I masturbated
asking me Do you take this woman for your lawful wedded wife?
And I trembling what to say say Pie Glue!
I kiss the bride all those corny men slapping me on the back

She's all yours, boy! Ha-ha-ha!
And in their eyes you could see some obscene honeymoon going on—
Then all that absurd rice and clanky cans and shoes
Niagara Falls! Hordes of us! Husbands! Wives! Flowers! Chocolates!
All streaming into cozy hotels
All going to do the same thing tonight
The indifferent clerk he knowing what was going to happen
The lobby zombies they knowing what
The whistling elevator man he knowing
The winking bellboy knowing
Everybody knowing! I'd be almost inclined not to do anything!
Stay up all night! Stare that hotel clerk in the eye!
Screaming: I deny honeymoon! I deny honeymoon!
running rampant into those almost climactic suites
yelling Radio belly! Cat shovel!
O I'd live in Niagara forever! in a dark cave beneath the Falls
I'd sit there the Mad Honeymooner
devising ways to break marriages, a scourge of bigamy
a saint of divorce—

But I should get married I should be good
How nice it'd be to come home to her
and sit by the fireplace and she in the kitchen
aproned young and lovely wanting my baby
and so happy about me she burns the roast beef
and comes crying to me and I get up from my big papa chair
saying Christmas teeth! Radiant brains! Apple deaf!
God what a husband I'd make! Yes, I should get married!
So much to do! like sneaking into Mr Jones' house late at night
and cover his golf clubs with 1920 Norwegian books
Like hanging a picture of Rimbaud on the lawnmower
like pasting Tannu Tuva postage stamps all over the picket fence
like when Mrs. Kindhead comes to collect for the Community Chest
grab her and tell her There are unfavorable omens in the sky!
And when the mayor comes to get my vote tell him
When are you going to stop people killing whales!
And when the milkman comes leave him a note in the bottle
Penguin dust, bring me penguin dust, I want penguin dust—

Yet if I should get married and it's Connecticut and snow
and she gives birth to a child and I am sleepless, worn,
up for nights, head bowed against a quiet window, the past behind me,
finding myself in the most common of situations a trembling man
knowledged with responsibility not twig-smear nor Roman coin soup—

O what would that be like!
Surely I'd give it for a nipple a rubber Tacitus
For a rattle a bag of broken Bach records
Tack Della Francesca all over its crib
Sew the Greek alphabet on its bib
And build for its playpen a roofless Parthenon

No, I doubt I'd be that kind of father
not rural not snow no quiet window
but hot smelly tight New York City
seven flights up, roaches and rats in the walls
a fat Reichian wife screeching over potatoes Get a job!
And five nose running brats in love with Batman
And the neighbors all toothless and dry haired
like those hag masses of the 18th century
all wanting to come in and watch TV
The landlord wants his rent
Grocery store Blue Cross Gas & Electric Knights of Columbus
Impossible to lie back and dream Telephone snow, ghost parking—
No! I should not get married I should never get married!
But—imagine if I were married to a beautiful sophisticated woman
tall and pale wearing an elegant black dress and long black gloves
holding a cigarette holder in one hand and a highball in the other
and we lived high up in a penthouse with a huge window
from which we could see all of New York and ever farther on clearer days
No, can't imagine myself married to that pleasant prison dream—

O but what about love? I forget love
not that I am incapable of love
it's just that I see love as odd as wearing shoes—
I never wanted to marry a girl who was like my mother
And Ingrid Bergman was always impossible
And there's maybe a girl now but she's already married
And I don't like men and—
but there's got to be somebody!
Because what if I'm 60 years old and not married,
all alone in a furnished room with pee stains on my underwear
and everybody else is married! All the universe married but me!

Ah, yet well I know that were a woman possible as I am possible
then marriage would be possible—
Like SHE in her lonely alien gaud waiting her Egyptian lover
so I wait—bereft of 2,000 years and the bath of life.

GARY SNYDER

Walt Whitman, whose vision of "democratic man" took form in his life as well as in his poems, would have seen Gary Snyder as a true son, just as Allen Ginsberg, another walker on Whitman's open road, recognized Snyder as a comrade. In September 1955, Ginsberg met

> a bearded interesting Berkeley cat name of Snyder, . . . who is studying oriental and leaving in a few months on some privately put up funds to go be a Zen monk (a real one). He's a head, peyotlist, laconist, but warmhearted, nice looking with a little beard, thin, blond, rides a bicycle in Berkeley in red corduroy and levis and hungup on Indians . . . Interesting person.*

Snyder has gone beyond being "an interesting person." Now in his forties, he has made of his life a pattern for survival. Through study of oriental and American Indian styles of life Snyder has learned and practiced ancient ways of living, thinking, and feeling. His diaries, published (together with several essays) as *Earth House Hold* (1969), show him moving outward in space and backward in time, slowly, methodically, like a farmer clearing a field, until he reaches a style of life that is deeply traditional yet wholly his own.

Ginsberg called him a laconist, a man of few words, and so he is. Many of his poems are very short; even when they are long ("Bubb's Creek Haircut"), they seem brief because the experiences they comment on are so large, full, and strongly felt. Also, many of Snyder's poems describe peaceful moments of understanding he has come to through work—and the weather and the place and the companions of the work—as if practical experience had helped him to cleanse his ideas and assay his words.

Gary Snyder, born 1930 in San Francisco, grew up on a farm north of Seattle:

> (At thirty-five my father had a wife,
> two children, two acres, and two cows.
> he built a barn, fixed the house and added on.
> strung barbed-wire fence,
> planted fruit-trees, blasted stumps.
> they always had a car.
> they thought they were poor—1935—)
> —IN THE NIGHT, FRIEND from *Regarding Wave*

At eighteen he shipped out of the port of New York as a seaman. At 21 he was graduated from Reed College (Portland, Oregon), his degree in anthropology and literature. After about a year at Indiana University, a center for the study of anthropology and folklore, he enrolled in the University of California, Berkeley, where he studied oriental languages for three years. In 1956 he went

---

*Ann Charters, ed., *Scenes Along the Road* (New York: Portents/Gotham Book Mart, 1970), p. 30.

to Japan (since then he has lived almost as much in Japan as in America). In 1960 and 1962 he lived and traveled in India. He visited many Buddhist communities and met the Dalai Lama in Tibet, with his second wife (Joanne Kyger, a poet) and friends. In 1964 he taught in the English department of the University of California, Berkeley.

In the late 1960s he was again in Japan, this time on a grant from the Bollingen Foundation to study Zen Buddhist training. In 1967 he married his third wife, Masa Uehara, a Japanese friend. At the time of the wedding they lived on Suwa-no-se Island, a small volcanic island, the home of forty villagers who fish, farm, and raise some pigs and goats. Snyder describes the wedding:

> The whole ashram* stayed up late the night before, packing a breakfast for the morrow. . . . We got up at 4:30 and started up the brush trail in the dark. First dipping into a ravine and then winding up a jungly knife-edge ridge. By five we were out of the jungle and onto a bare lava slope. Following the long ridge to an older, extinct crater and on to the crest of the main crater and the summit shortly after sunrise. The lip of the crater drops off into cloud; and out of the cloud comes a roaring like an airport full of jets: a billowing of steam upwards. The cloud and the mist broke, and we could see 800 feet or so down into the crater—at least a mile across—and fumaroles and steam-jets; at the very center red molten lava in a little bubbly pond. . . .
>
> Standing on the edge of the crater, blowing the conch horn and chanting a mantra; offering shochu to the gods of the volcano, the ocean, and the sky; then Masa and I exchanged the traditional three sips—Pon and Nanao said a few words; Masa and I spoke; we recited the Four Vows together, and ended with three blasts on the conch. Got out of the wind and opened the ruck sacks to eat the food made the night before. . . . We descended from the summit and were down to the Banyan tree by eleven—went direct on out to the ocean and into the water; so that within one morning we passed from the windy volcanic summit to the warm coral waters. At four in the afternoon all the villagers came to the ashram. . . . Pretty soon everyone was singing Amami folksongs and doing traditional dances.*

Snyder and his family now live in northern California.

As in "primitive" communities, each part of Snyder's life is connected closely with the whole—work, politics, philosophy, food, esthetics, sex, and poetry. Snyder aims to live as much as possible above the typical Western system of divisions and separations of mind and body, action and contemplation, self and world, and individual and society. When Snyder describes how his poems are made, one sees how closely, for him, art and life work together.

For Snyder, as for many poets, experience gives rise to a poem, and the poem clarifies the experience. To state the relationship between experience

*An ashram is a religious retreat for a colony of disciples.
*Earth House Hold (New York: New Directions, 1969), p. 142.

and poetry in this way is to utter a truism, but few poets have put into poetry experiences so physical, sensory, and concrete as Snyder's, and rarely have poetic forms and rhythms come from such physical experience. Perhaps only a very few poets have had Snyder's wide experience of physical labor upon which to draw. In 1960 Snyder explained how he makes his poems:

> I've . . . come to realize that the rhythms of my poems follow the rhythm of the physical work I'm doing and life I'm leading at any given time—which makes the music in my head which creates, the line. Conditioned by the poetic tradition of the English language and whatever feelings I have for the sound of poems I dig in other languages.*

Several poems included here illustrate how the form and rhythm of Snyder's poems grow out of work or physical experience. "Mid-August at Sourdough Mountain Lookout," "Hay for the Horses," and "For a Far-out Friend" come from a collection of poems called *Riprap and Cold Mountain Poems*. Riprap is "a cobble of stone laid on steep slick rock to make a trail for horses in the mountains."† These poems, Snyder explains, were made under the influence of doing trail work in the high Sierra. The title word itself turns action into poetry. "Riprap," the sound of rock on rock, belongs to a class of words called onomatopoeic—words like "buzz," "crack," and "bow-wow" that imitate sounds. It is a word that Snyder learned in the Sierra from a man, not a book. He writes of these poems

> "Riprap" is . . . a class of poems I wrote under the influence of the geology of the Sierra Nevada and the daily trail-crew work of picking up and placing granite stones in tight cobble patterns on hard slab. "What are you doing?" I asked old Roy Marchbanks. —"Riprapping," he said. His selection of natural rocks was perfect—the result looked like dressed stone fitting to hair-edge cracks. Walking, climbing, placing with the hands. I tried writing poems of tough, simple, short words, with the complexity far beneath the surface texture. In part the line was influenced by the five- and seven-character-line Chinese poems I'd been reading, which work like sharp blows on the mind.*

In his most recent collection of poems, *Regarding Wave,* many rhythms and images are taken from the sea, from the sound and feel of waves and wind, and from the movements of sexual life. The title poem, "Wave," praises (and imitates) curves and undulating motions in waves, trees, rocks, and women.

Ezra Pound wrote that "artists are the antennae of the race."† The metaphor fits Snyder. He is a man delicately exploring the endless border between present

---

*Quoted in Donald M. Allen, ed., *The New American Poetry: 1945-1960* (New York: Grove Press, 1960), p. 420.

†From the title page of *Riprap and Cold Mountain Poems* (San Francisco: Four Seasons Foundation, 1965).

*The New American Poetry, p. 421.

†*ABC of Reading* (New York: New Directions, 1960), p. 81. (First published 1934.)

and past, between filthy Tokyo and Suwa-no-se Island. He is a sensor, a listener, and he takes note of dangers. He knows, for example

> Something is always eating at the American heart like acid: it is the knowledge of what we have done to our continent, and to the American Indian.
> Other civilizations have done the same, but at a pace too slow to be remembered.‡

One does not need an apparatus as sensitive as Snyder's to know this. Snyder's great value is not to warn but to find ways out. He knows something of religion as "the vehicle of hair-raising liberating and healing realizations"; he has explored "the mind in its untamed state as distinct from mind cultivated or domesticated for yielding a return"; he has lived with community as a "knowledge of connection and responsibility"; and he knows poetry as a voice that "speaks through you clearer and stronger than what you know of yourself, with a sureness and melody of its own, singing out the inner song of the self, and of the planet."* In *Earth House Hold* there is an essay on the usefulness of poetry entitled "Poetry and the Primitive: Notes on Poetry as an Ecological Survival Technique." When Gary Snyder calls poetry a survival technique, he speaks prophetically, as well as from his own experience.

The poems are from *Riprap and Cold Mountain Poems* (1965), *Six Sections from Mountains and Rivers Without End* (1965), *Back Country* (1968), and *Regarding Wave* (1970).

---

‡"Poetry and the Primitive: Notes on Poetry as an Ecological Survival Technique," *Earth House Hold,* p. 119.
*"Poetry and the Primitive," *Earth House Hold,* p. 123. The phrase "the mind in its untamed state as distinct from mind cultivated or domesticated for yielding a return" is from Claude Lévi-Strauss, *The Savage Mind.*

FOR A FAR-OUT FRIEND

Because I once beat you up
Drunk, stung with weeks of torment
And saw you no more,
And you had calm talk for me today
           I now suppose
I was less sane than you,
You hung on dago red,
              me hooked on books.
You once ran naked toward me
Knee deep in cold March surf
On a tricky beach between two
            pounding seastacks—
I saw you as a Hindu Deva-girl[1]
Light legs dancing in the waves,
Breasts like dream-breasts
Of sea, and child, and astral
           Venus-spurting milk.
And traded our salt lips.

Visions of your body
Kept me high for weeks, I even had
           a sort of trance for you
A day in a dentist's chair.
I found you again, gone stone,
In Zimmer's book of Indian Art:
Dancing in that life with
Grace and love, with rings
And a little golden belt, just above
             your naked snatch
And I thought—more grace and love
In that wild Deva life where you belong
Than in this dress-and-girdle life
You'll ever give
Or get.

                    1955

[1] *Hindu Deva-girl* a deva is a divine being or God (Hinduism, Buddhism); devadasis are "brides of the Gods," that is, temple prostitutes.

MARIN-AN[1]

sun breaks over the eucalyptus
grove below the wet pasture,
water's about hot,
I sit in the open window
& roll a smoke.

distant dogs bark, a pair of
cawing crows; the twang
of a pygmy nuthatch high in a pine—
from behind the cypress windrow
the mare moves up, grazing.

a soft continuous roar
comes out of the far valley
of the six-lane highway—thousands
and thousands of cars
driving men to work.

1956

[1] *Marin-An* Marin County lies north of San Francisco, across the Golden Gate Bridge from the city.

MID-AUGUST AT SOURDOUGH MOUNTAIN LOOKOUT

Down valley a smoke haze
Three days heat, after five days rain
Pitch glows in the fir-cones
Across rocks and meadows
Swarms of new flies.

I cannot remember things I once read
A few friends, but they are in cities.
Drinking cold snow-water from a tin cup
Looking down for miles
Through high still air.

HAY FOR THE HORSES

He had driven half the night
From far down San Joaquin
Through Mariposa, up the
Dangerous mountain roads,
And pulled in at eight a.m.
With his big truckload of hay
           behind the barn.
With winch and ropes and hooks
We stacked the bales up clean
To splintery redwood rafters
High in the dark, flecks of alfalfa
Whirling through shingle-cracks of light,
Itch of haydust in the
           sweaty shirt and shoes.
At lunchtime under Black oak
Out in the hot corral,
—The old mare nosing lunchpails,
Grasshoppers crackling in the weeds—
"I'm sixty-eight" he said,
"I first bucked hay when I was seventeen.
I thought, that day I started,
I sure would hate to do this all my life.
And dammit, that's just what
I've gone and done."

                        1957

BUBBS CREEK HAIRCUT

for Locke McCorkle

High ceilingd and the double mirrors, the
        calendar a splendid alpine scene—scab barber—
in stained white barber gown, alone, sat down, old man
A summer fog gray San Francisco day
I walked right in. on Howard street
                    haircut a dollar twenty-five.
Just clip it close as it will go.
    "now why you want your hair cut back like that."
    —well I'm going to the Sierras for a while

Bubbs Creek and on across to upper Kern.
                    he wriggled clippers,
"Well I been up there, I built the cabin
    up at Cedar Grove. In nineteen five."
                            old haircut smell

Next door, Goodwill.¹
                    where I came out.
A search for sweater, and a stroll
                in the board & concrete room of
                    unfixed junk downstair—
All emblems of the past—too close—
    heaped up in chilly dust and bare bulb glare
Of tables, wheelchairs, battered trunks & wheels
& pots that boiled up coffee nineteen ten, *things*
Swimming on their own & finally freed
                        from human need. Or?
        waiting a final flicker of desire
To tote them out once more. Some freakish use.
The Master of the limbo drag-leggd watches
                            making prices
            to the people seldom buy
The sag-assd rocker has to make it now. Alone.

            A few weeks later drove with Locke
    down San Joaquin, us barefoot in the heat
    stopping for beer & melon on the way
                        the Giant Orange,
    rubber shreds of cast truck retreads on the pebble
    shoulders, highway ninety-nine.
                    Sierras marked by cumulus
                    in the east.
    car coughing in the groves, six thousand feet;
    down to Kings River Canyon; camped at Cedar Grove.
                hard granite canyon walls that
                leave no scree

Once tried a haircut at the Barber College too—
Sat half an hour before they told me
                white men use the other side.
Goodwill, St. Vincent de Paul,
            Salvation Army, up the coast
For mackinaws and boots and heavy socks

     —Seattle has the best for logger gear
Once found a pair of good tricouni
    at the under-the-public-market store,
    Mark Tobey's scene,[2]
      torn down I hear—
& Filson jacket with a birdblood stain.

A. G. & me got winter clothes for almost nothing
   at Lake Union, telling the old gal
    we was on our way
To work the winter out up in B. C.
        hitch-hiking home the
Green hat got a ride (of that more later)

   hiking up Bubbs creek saw the trail crew tent
   in a scraggly grove of creekside lodgepole pine
       talked to the guy, he says
   "If you see McCool on the other trailcrew over there
   tell him Moorehead says to go to hell."

   late snow that summer. Crossing the scarred bare
       shed of Forester Pass
    the winding rock-braced switchbacks
   dive in snowbanks, we climb on where
      pack trains have to dig or wait.
   a half iced-over lake, twelve thousand feet
      its sterile boulder bank
   but filled with leaping trout:
      reflections wobble in the
   mingling circles always spreading out
     the crazy web of wavelets makes sense
     seen from high above.
   the realm of fallen rock.
   a deva world[3] of sorts—it's high
      it is a view that few men see, a point
    bare sunlight
    on the spaces
   empty sky
      moulding to fit the shape of what ice left
   of fire-thrust, or of tilted, twisted, faulted
      cast-out from this lava belly globe.

The boulder in my minds eye is a chair.

```
                    . . . why was the man drag legg'd?
King of Hell
                    or is it a paradise of sorts, thus freed
From acting out the function some
                                        creator/carpenter
Thrust on a thing to think he made, himself,
                    an object always "chair"
                                        Sinister ritual histories.
                is the Mountain God a gimp?
"le Roi Boeuf" and the ritual limp?
                                    Good   Will?


Daughter of mountains, stoopd
                moon breast Parvati⁴
  mountain thunder speaks
  hair tingling static as the lightning lashes
  is neither word of love or wisdom;
  though this be danger:   hence thee fear.
                        Some flowing girl
  whose slippery dance
  entrances Shiva
                —the valley spirit/ Anahita,
                                Sarasvati,⁵
  dark and female gate of all the world
  water that cuts back quartzflake sand
                        Soft is the dance that melts the
  mat-haired mountain sitter
                to leap in fire
  & make of sand a tree
        of tree a board, of board (ideas!)
        somebody's rocking chair.
  a room of empty sun of peaks and ridges
        beautiful spirits,
                        rocking lotus throne:
  a universe of junk, all left alone.
```

The hat I always take on mountains:
When we came back down through Oregon
                            (three years before)
At nightfall in the Siskiyou⁶ few cars pass
A big truck stopped a hundred yards above
        "Siskiyou Stoneware" on the side
The driver said

He recognized my old green hat.
I'd had a ride
            with him two years before
A whole state north
            when hitching down to Portland
                      from Warm Springs.[7]
  Allen in the rear on straw
    forgot salami   and we went on south
  all night—in many cars—to Berkeley in the dawn.

      upper Kern River country now after nine days walk
    it finally rain.
        we ran on that other trail crew
    setting up new camp in the drizzly pine
    cussing & slapping bugs, 4 days from road,
    we saw McCool, & he said tell that Moorehead
        KISS MY ASS
    we squatted smoking by the fire.
        "I'll never get a green hat now"
    the foreman says   fifty mosquitoes sitting on the brim
                      they must like green.
    & two more days of thundershower and cold
        (on Whitney[8] hair on end
        hail stinging barelegs in the blast of wind
        but yodel off the summit echoes clean)

        all this came after:
Purity of the mountains and goodwills.
The diamond drill of racing icemelt waters
        and bumming trucks & watching
Buildings raze
        the garbage acres burning at the Bay
        the girl who was the skid-row
Cripple's daughter—

            out of the memory of smoking pine
The lotion and the spittoon glitter rises

Chair turns and in the double mirror waver
The old man cranks me down and cracks a chuckle

"your Bubbs Creek haircut, boy."

1961

¹*Goodwill* a store for the resale of used things, staffed by handicapped persons. ²Mark Tobey (b. 1890), a painter known for his squiggly calligraphic style of abstract expressionism. ³*deva world* a divine world of the gods and good spirits (Hinduism, Buddhism). ⁴*Parvati* Hindu goddess of love, maternity, and death and consort of Shiva. Shiva, the destroyer, is one of the Hindu triad, together with Brahma the creator and Vishnu the preserver. ⁵*Anahita, Sarasvati* the Hindu goddess of learning and the arts. ⁶*Siskiyou* a forest and mountain range in Oregon. ⁷*Warm Springs* a town and Indian reservation in Oregon. ⁸*Whitney* Mt. Whitney, the highest peak (14,495 feet) in the Sierra Nevada.

WHAT YOU SHOULD KNOW TO BE A POET

all you can about animals as persons.
the names of trees and flowers and weeds.
names of stars, and the movements of the planets
     and the moon.

your own six senses, with a watchful and elegant mind.

at least one kind of traditional magic:
divination, astrology, the *book of changes*,¹ the tarot;²

dreams.
the illusory demons and illusory shining gods;

kiss the ass of the devil and eat shit;
fuck his horny barbed cock,
fuck the hag,
and all the celestial angels
    and maidens perfum'd and golden—

& then love the human: wives husbands and friends.

childrens' games, comic books, bubble-gum,
the weirdness of television and advertising.

work, long dry hours of dull work swallowed and accepted
and livd with and finally lovd.   exhaustion,
                    hunger, rest.

the wild freedom of the dance, *extasy*
silent solitary illumination, *enstasy*

real danger.   gambles.   and the edge of death.

                                                    1965

   [1]*The book of changes* an ancient Chinese book of divination, also called the *I Ching*.
[2]*the tarot* a set of pictorial cards used in fortune-telling.

WAVE

    Grooving clam shell,
           streakt through marble,
       sweeping down ponderosa pine bark-scale
         rip-cut[1] tree grain
              sand-dunes, lava
                  flow

Wave   wife.
             woman—wyfman[2]—
"veiled; vibrating; vague"
   sawtooth ranges pulsing;
               veins on the back of the hand.

Forkt out: birdsfoot-alluvium
                  wash

      great dunes rolling
Each inch rippld, every grain a wave.

Leaning against sand cornices til they blow away

```
    —wind, shake
    stiff thorns of cholla, ocotillo
    sometimes I get stuck in thickets—
```

Ah, trembling spreading radiating wyf
                            racing zebra
   catch me and fling me wide
To the dancing grain of things
                            of my mind!

                                    1966

¹*rip-cut* sawed along the grain of the wood. ²*wyfman* (Old English) "woman."

SONG OF THE TASTE

Eating the living germs of grasses
Eating the ova of large birds

   the fleshy sweetness packed
   around the sperm of swaying trees

The muscles of the flanks and thighs of
            soft-voiced cows
   the bounce in the lamb's leap
   the swish in the ox's tail

Eating roots grown swoll
            inside the soil

Drawing on life of living
     clustered points of light spun
            out of space
hidden in the grape.

Eating each other's seed
            eating
   ah, each other.

Kissing the lover in the mouth of bread:
            lip to lip.

                        1966

REVOLUTION IN THE REVOLUTION IN THE REVOLUTION

The country surrounds the city
The back country surrounds the country

"From the masses to the masses" the most
Revolutionary consciousness is to be found
Among the most ruthlessly exploited classes:
Animals, trees, water, air, grasses

We must pass through the stage of the
"Dictatorship of the Unconscious" before we can
Hope for the withering-away of the states
And finally arrive at true Communionism.

If the capitalists and imperialists
      are the exploiters, the masses are the workers.
         and the party
         is the communist.

If civilization
      is the exploiter, the masses is nature.
         and the party
         is the poets.

If the abstract rational intellect
      is the exploiter, the masses is the unconscious.
         and the party
         is the yogins.

& POWER
comes out of the seed-syllables of mantras.

1968

LONG HAIR

Hunting season:

Once every year, the Deer catch human beings. They
do various things which irresistibly draw men near them;
each one selects a certain man. The Deer shoots the man,

who is then compelled to skin it and carry its meat home
and eat it. Then the Deer is inside the man. He waits
and hides in there, but the man doesn't know it. When
enough Deer have occupied enough men, they will strike
all at once. The men who don't have Deer in them will
also be taken by surprise, and everything will change
some. This is called "takeover from inside."

Deer trails:

Deer trails run on the side hills
        cross country access roads
        dirt ruts to bone-white
        board house ranches,
        tumbled down.

Waist high through manzanita,
Through sticky, prickly, crackling
        gold dry summer grass.

Deer trails lead to water,
Lead sidewise all ways
Narrowing down to one best path—
And split—
And fade away to nowhere.

Deer trails slide under freeways
        slip into cities
        swing back and forth in crops and orchards
        run up the sides of schools!

Deer spoor and crisscross dusty tracks
Are in the house: and coming out the walls:

And deer bound through my hair.

1968

SYLVIA PLATH

The reputation of Sylvia Plath, which now stands very high, rests mainly upon one volume of poetry, *Ariel* (1965). Another gathering of poems, *The Colossus* (1960), illustrates her inventiveness and the authority of her style, and an autobiographical novel, *The Bell Jar* (1963), published under the pseudonym Victoria Lucas, contains brilliant satiric comedy.* Still, the poems she wrote during the last year of her life between the birth of her son in January 1962 and her suicide in February 1963 supply the abiding excellence and the proof of poetic growth that have won her admiration, respect, and prize of prizes, the haloed word "genius."

Success, even the solid and respectable kind that was hers, stands far apart from the personal life of thought and feeling. Yet Sylvia Plath should not be remembered with pity as a pathetic success, as an "unhappy genius." The true curve of her life is the line of ambition, energy, self-discovery, courage, and (what is both uncommon and essential) disciplined competence to express what she knew of herself.

Sylvia Plath's father, Otto, a German born in Poland, died when she was just eight. (She was born in Boston in 1932.) He had been a professor of biology at Boston University, an authority on bees, a learned and altogether impressive man. In Sylvia Plath's words, "Her father died while she thought he was God."†

Sylvia Plath's mother, Aurelia Schober, also came from a German background. Her parents were emigrants from Austria. When she met her husband, she was studying German literature. After his death she took up a humble sort of teaching at Boston University. She taught secretarial skills to students in a program for medical secretaries. If her daughter's description in *The Bell Jar* is truthful, she hated the work. She bought a new house to share with her parents after her husband's death. Before, both families had lived very near the sea, but the death of Otto Plath meant leaving the shore to move to Wellesley, Massachusetts, a suburb of Boston.

Sylvia went to Smith College. She graduated with highest academic honors and won many prizes for her creative work. One of those prizes was a summer of work in New York City (1953) as a guest editor with *Mademoiselle* magazine. At the end of the summer she returned home, peculiar and depressed. She tried then to kill herself, hiding away under the house and swallowing some fifty sleeping pills, but she was found by chance after she had lain unconscious

---

*Two other volumes have since appeared, *Crossing the Water* (1971) and *Winter Trees* (1972).

†Sylvia Plath describes the speaker of the poem "Daddy" with these words. She had prepared notes on this poem and several others for "New Poems," a reading to have been broadcast on the BBC Third Programme. A. Alvarez quoted from her notes in "Sylvia Plath," a memorial broadcast on the BBC Third Programme, printed, with additions, in *Tri-Quarterly* (Fall, 1966), and reprinted in Charles Newman, ed., *The Art of Sylvia Plath* (Bloomington: Indiana University Press, 1970), p. 65.

for a long time. She recovered in a mental hospital and returned to college. When she graduated (1955) she was awarded a Fulbright grant to study in England. There, at Cambridge University, she met Ted Hughes, a poet of great talent, and in June 1956 they were married. She returned to Smith College to teach (1957-1958), but she chose not to continue that career—too many themes to correct, too little time to write.

She and her husband later returned to England. A first child, Frieda, was born in April 1960; a second, Nicholas, in January 1962. By autumn of 1962 she and her husband were separated. She and the children spent Christmas alone in London. That winter was bitter cold, reportedly the coldest winter in 150 years. On February 11, 1963, she succeeded in taking her life. Several details seem to suggest that she hoped again to be rescued, to be discovered in time, though unconscious from gas, by a young woman who was supposed to care for the children that morning.* She wrote of suicide as her fate ("Edge," "Words"), but her death seems more an accident of despair.

Sylvia Plath's development as a poet is orderly, if one grants that great excellence is always a surprise. Her early poems, represented here by "All the Dead Dears," "The Colossus," and "Night Shift," were written slowly, laboriously, while she made constant reference to a thesaurus that had belonged to her father.* These poems are dense and difficult, although like all her work they are clear and intelligible when one reads them slowly, with the mind. In speaking of the poems in *The Colossus,* her first book, she said, "I can't read any of the poems aloud now. I didn't write them to be read aloud. In fact, they quite privately bore me."† Of her later poems ("Lady Lazarus" and "Daddy" among them) she spoke with positive assurance: "Now these very recent ones—I've got to say them. I speak them to myself. Whatever lucidity they may have comes from the fact that I say them aloud."‡

The later poems are more lucid and more powerful than the earlier ones. In several ways they are simpler. The poems in *The Colossus* reveal only indistinctly the expressive impulse behind the poem, whereas the later ones tell much more about her feelings and what it was that hurt in her. "The Colossus" is the same man as "Daddy," but a reader could understand the first poem to be an exercise of the imagination, a dramatic monologue spoken by Agamemnon's daughter Electra. The earlier poems keep the promise she makes in "The Disquieting Muses," a poem about her "companions'" uneasiness, a sense of doom and a threat of violence:

---

*See A. Alvarez, "Sylvia Plath: A Memoir," *New American Review, 12* (1971), 37-39.

*Ted Hughes, "Notes on the Chronological Order of Sylvia Plath's Poems," in *The Art of Sylvia Plath,* ed. Charles Newman, p. 188.
†Quoted by A. Alvarez in "Sylvia Plath," in Charles Newman, ed., *The Art of Sylvia Plath,* p. 59.
‡*The Art of Sylvia Plath,* p. 59.

> But no frown of mine
> Will betray the company I keep.

Later she spoke directly of the anger and the death-sickness that grew in her, as if, as she put it in "Kindness" (not included here)

> The blood jet is poetry,
> There is no stopping it.

The later poems are simpler in formal ways; they are less "busy." Although all Sylvia Plath's poems stand upon her disciplined literary training and exercise, the later ones contain fewer references to literature, and stanza forms and rhyme schemes are less obviously present. Throughout her poems the metaphors are brilliant—exact, accurate, and surprising—but in the later poems the pace has changed: on the whole there are fewer metaphors.

The rhymes and rhythms of the later poems can't be described easily as "simpler." She continued to use many off-rhymes, like "grow" and "furrow" or "flies" and "drive" in "Ariel." In *Ariel,* as in *The Colossus,* are many poems that do not rhyme at all, but that are linked by echoes of small units of sound ("fine" and "linen" in "Lady Lazarus"). On the other hand, some of the later poems are more heavily rhymed than any of the early ones ("do," "shoe," "Achoo," and "you" in "Daddy"). The changes could mean that she felt more free to follow the irrational surge of the poem, *her* poem, and the sound of a voice, *her* voice. The rhythms of the later poems are loose, moving toward a rhythm roughly iambic or toward clusters of anapests (◡ ◡ —). A poem like "You're," written in lines measured mainly by syllable count, fits better in *The Colossus* than in *Ariel.* It is an early poem (March 1960), written during her first pregnancy. (The poem was written in the eighth month of her pregnancy. Most lines contain eight syllables, and each stanza has nine lines.)

Like the poems of T.S. Eliot that were so popular during the fifties when she was in college, her early poems are elegant, artful, learned, and intellectual. The later poems, too, are elegant and intellectually solid; but they are also shocking and overwhelming, poems to be read aloud in anger or in sorrow, or in a wild, desperate joy.

> Dying
> Is an art, like everything else.
> I do it exceptionally well.
>
> I do it so it feels like hell.
> —LADY LAZARUS

> Daddy, daddy, you bastard, I'm through.
> —DADDY

And I
Am the arrow,

The dew that flies
Suicidal, at one with the drive
Into the red

Eye, the cauldron of morning.
—ARIEL

Sylvia Plath has moved closer to the poem to be said or chanted, the poem written to express powerful emotions openly and nakedly. Allen Ginsberg is the great man of the voice, of the public performance of private life; but the poet who helped Sylvia Plath to speak with a dramatic, personal voice was Robert Lowell—who, like her and before her, changed his style. Lowell moved from intricate, formal verse toward speech rhythms and common language. At the same time he began to write more and more fully of himself and his family (*Life Studies,* 1959). Sylvia Plath discovered in herself a marvelous dramatic voice (she did write a radio play for the BBC).* One wishes that she could have invented tragic characters.

We must remind ourselves that suffering does not make poems. The difference between "The Colossus" and "Daddy" is not that she suffered more when she wrote the latter. At nineteen, long before she had written either poem, she was ready to die. The later poems come from her courage to say what she felt, but even more, from her discipline as an artist, from patient work with metaphor, rhyme, and rhythm, and from her willingness to write again and again on similar subjects in order to perfect a vocabulary of words and images (stones, blood, bone, the moon, and water are some of them).

The poems are printed, as much as possible, in chronological order, though the dates are sometimes approximate.

---

*Three Women, 1962. An excerpt appears in *The Art of Sylvia Plath,* pp. 261-65. The speakers are three women in a hospital. One has given birth to a boy, one to a girl (whom she rejects), and one has miscarried.

ALL THE DEAD DEARS

In the Archaeological Museum in Cambridge is a stone coffin of the fourth century A.D. containing the skeletons of a woman, a mouse and a shrew. The ankle-bone of the woman has been slightly gnawn.

Rigged poker-stiff on her back
With a granite grin
This antique museum-cased lady
Lies, companioned by the gimcrack
Relics of a mouse and a shrew
That battened for a day on her ankle-bone.

These three, unmasked now, bear
Dry witness
To the gross eating game
We'd wink at if we didn't hear
Stars grinding, crumb by crumb,
Our own grist down to its bony face.

How they grip us through thin and thick,
These barnacle dead!
This lady here's no kin
Of mine, yet kin she is: she'll suck
Blood and whistle my marrow clean
To prove it. As I think now of her head,

From the mercury-backed glass
Mother, grandmother, greatgrandmother
Reach hag hands to haul me in,
And an image looms under the fishpond
      surface
Where the daft father went down
With orange duck-feet winnowing his
      hair—

All the long gone darlings: they
Get back, though, soon,
Soon: be it by wakes, weddings,
Childbirths or a family barbecue:

Any touch, taste, tang's
Fit for those outlaws to ride home on,

And to sanctuary: usurping the armchair
Between tick
And tack of the clock, until we go,
Each skulled-and-crossboned Gulliver
Riddled with ghosts, to lie
Deadlocked with them, taking root as
      cradles rock.

1956

THE DISQUIETING MUSES[1]

Mother, mother, what illbred aunt
Or what disfigured and unsightly
Cousin did you so unwisely keep
Unasked to my christening, that she
Sent these ladies in her stead
With heads like darning-eggs to nod
And nod and nod at foot and head
And at the left side of my crib?

Mother, who made to order stories
Of Mixie Blackshort the heroic bear,
Mother, whose witches always, always
Got baked into gingerbread, I wonder
Whether you saw them, whether you said
Words to rid me of those three ladies
Nodding by night around my bed,
Mouthless, eyeless, with stitched bald head.

In the hurricane, when father's twelve
Study windows bellied in
Like bubbles about to break, you fed
My brother and me cookies and Ovaltine
And helped the two of us to choir:
"Thor is angry: boom boom boom!
Thor is angry: we don't care!"
But those ladies broke the panes.

When on tiptoe the schoolgirls danced,
Blinking flashlights like fireflies
And singing the glowworm song, I could
Not lift a foot in the twinkle-dress
But, heavy-footed, stood aside
In the shadow cast by my dismal-headed
Godmothers, and you cried and cried:
And the shadow stretched, the lights went out.

Mother, you sent me to piano lessons
And praised my arabesques and trills
Although each teacher found my touch
Oddly wooden in spite of scales
And the hours of practicing, my ear
Tone-deaf and yes, unteachable.
I learned, I learned, I learned elsewhere,
From muses unhired by you, dear mother,

I woke one day to see you, mother,
Floating above me in bluest air
On a green balloon bright with a million
Flowers and bluebirds that never were
Never, never, found anywhere.
But the little planet bobbed away
Like a soap-bubble as you called: Come here!
And I faced my traveling companions.

Day now, night now, at head, side, feet,
They stand their vigil in gowns of stone,
Faces blank as the day I was born,
Their shadows long in the setting sun
That never brightens or goes down.
And this is the kingdom you bore me to,
Mother, mother. But no frown of mine
Will betray the company I keep.

1957-1958

[1]*The Disquieting Muses* The Muses are Greek goddesses who inspire poets and others to great work. In fairy tales the heroine is sometimes cursed by a fairy or witch who is angry because she was not invited to the christening party.

NIGHT SHIFT

It was not a heart, beating,
That muted boom, that clangor
Far off, not blood in the ears
Drumming up any fever

To impose on the evening.
The noise came from the outside:
A metal detonating
Native, evidently, to

These stilled suburbs: nobody
Startled at it, though the sound
Shook the ground with its pounding.
It took root at my coming

Till the thudding source, exposed,
Confounded inept guesswork:
Framed in windows of Main Street's
Silver factory, immense

Hammers hoisted, wheels turning,
Stalled, let fall their vertical
Tonnage of metal and wood;
Stunned the marrow. Men in white

Undershirts circled, tending
Without stop those greased machines,
Tending, without stop, the blunt
Indefatigable fact.

1957-1958

THE COLOSSUS[1]

I shall never get you put together entirely,
Pieced, glued, and properly jointed.
Mule-bray, pig-grunt and bawdy cackles
Proceed from your great lips.
It's worse than a barnyard.

Perhaps you consider yourself an oracle,
Mouthpiece of the dead, or of some god or other.
Thirty years now I have labored
To dredge the silt from your throat.
I am none the wiser.

Scaling little ladders with gluepots and pails of lysol
I crawl like an ant in mourning
Over the weedy acres of your brow
To mend the immense skull plates and clear
The bald, white tumuli of your eyes.

A blue sky out of the Oresteia[2]
Arches above us. O father, all by yourself
You are pithy and historical as the Roman Forum.
I open my lunch on a hill of black cypress.
Your fluted bones and acanthine hair are littered
In their old anarchy to the horizon-line.
It would take more than a lightning-stroke
To create such a ruin.
Nights, I squat in the cornucopia
Of your left ear, out of the wind,

Counting the red stars and those of plum-color.
The sun rises under the pillar of your tongue.
My hours are married to shadow.
No longer do I listen for the scrape of a keel
On the blank stones of the landing.

1958-1959

[1]*The Colossus.* One of the Seven Wonders of the Ancient World was a huge statue of Apollo called the Colossus that stood at the entrance to the harbor of the ancient Greek city of Rhodes. [2]*The Oresteia* is the name given to a series of plays by the Greek playwright Aeschylus (525-456 B.C.)—*Agamemnon, The Choephore,* and *The Eumenides*—about King Agamemnon's murder by his wife, and the subsequent revenge of his two children, Electra and Orestes. Orestes is driven mad because he has slain his mother. (Agamemnon was a hero of the Greek expedition against Troy.)

YOU'RE

Clownlike, happiest on your hands,
Feet to the stars, and moon-skulled,

Gilled like a fish. A common-sense
Thumbs-down on the dodo's mode.
Wrapped up in yourself like a spool,
Trawling your dark as owls do.
Mute as a turnip from the Fourth
Of July to All Fools' Day,
O high-riser, my little loaf.

Vague as fog and looked for like mail.
Farther off than Australia.
Bent-backed Atlas, our travelled prawn.
Snug as a bud and at home
Like a sprat in a pickle jug.
A creel of eels, all ripples.
Jumpy as a Mexican bean.
Right, like a well-done sum.
A clean slate, with your own face on.

March 1960

TULIPS[1]

The tulips are too excitable, it is winter here.
Look how white everything is, how quiet, how snowed-in.
I am learning peacefulness, lying by myself quietly
As the light lies on these white walls, this bed, these hands.
I am nobody; I have nothing to do with explosions.
I have given my name and my day-clothes up to the nurses
And my history to the anaesthetist and my body to surgeons.

They have propped my head between the pillow and the sheet-cuff
Like an eye between two white lids that will not shut.
Stupid pupil, it has to take everything in.
The nurses pass and pass, they are no trouble,
They pass the way gulls pass inland in their white caps,
Doing things with their hands, one just the same as another,
So it is impossible to tell how many there are.

My body is a pebble to them, they tend it as water
Tends to the pebbles it must run over, smoothing them gently.
They bring me numbness in their bright needles, they bring me sleep.
Now I have lost myself I am sick of baggage—

My patent leather overnight case like a black pillbox,
My husband and child smiling out of the family photo;
Their smiles catch onto my skin, little smiling hooks.

I have let things slip, a thirty-year-old cargo boat
Stubbornly hanging on to my name and address.
They have swabbed me clear of my loving associations.
Scared and bare on the green plastic-pillowed trolley
I watched my teaset, my bureaus of linen, my books
Sink out of sight, and the water went over my head.
I am a nun now, I have never been so pure.

I didn't want any flowers, I only wanted
To lie with my hands turned up and be utterly empty.
How free it is, you have no idea how free—
The peacefulness is so big it dazes you,
And it asks nothing, a name tag, a few trinkets.
It is what the dead close on, finally; I imagine them
Shutting their mouths on it, like a Communion tablet.

The tulips are too red in the first place, they hurt me.
Even through the gift paper I could hear them breathe
Lightly, through their white swaddlings, like an awful baby.
Their redness talks to my wound, it corresponds.
They are subtle: they seem to float, though they weigh me down,
Upsetting me with their sudden tongues and their colour,
A dozen red lead sinkers round my neck.

Nobody watched me before, now I am watched.
The tulips turn to me, and the window behind me
Where once a day the light slowly widens and slowly thins,
And I see myself, flat, ridiculous, a cut-paper shadow
Between the eye of the sun and the eyes of the tulips,
And I have no face, I have wanted to efface myself.
The vivid tulips eat my oxygen.

Before they came the air was calm enough,
Coming and going, breath by breath, without any fuss.
Then the tulips filled it up like a loud noise.
Now the air snags and eddies round them the way a river
Snags and eddies round a sunken rust-red engine.
They concentrate my attention, that was happy
Playing and resting without committing itself.

The walls, also, seem to be warming themselves.
The tulips should be behind bars like dangerous animals;
They are opening like the mouth of some great African cat,
And I am aware of my heart: it opens and closes
Its bowl of red blooms out of sheer love of me.
The water I taste is warm and salt, like the sea,
And comes from a country far away as health.

March 1961

¹In March 1961 Sylvia Plath had an appendectomy shortly after a miscarriage.

ARIEL¹

Stasis in darkness.
Then the substanceless blue
Pour of tor and distances.

God's lioness,
How one we grow,
Pivot of heels and knees!—The furrow

Splits and passes, sister to
The brown arc
Of the neck I cannot catch,

Nigger-eye
Berries cast dark
Hooks—

Black sweet blood mouthfuls,
Shadows.
Something else

Hauls me through air—
Thighs, hair;
Flakes from my heels.

White
Godiva, I unpeel—
Dead hands, dead stringencies.

And now I
Foam to wheat, a glitter of seas.
The child's cry

Melts in the wall.
And I
Am the arrow,

The dew that flies
Suicidal, at one with the drive
Into the red

Eye, the cauldron of morning.

    October-November 1962

 [1]*Ariel* The name of a noble and airy spirit in Shakespeare's play *The Tempest,* Ariel is also the name of a horse Sylvia Plath often rode. The poem recalls, too, a horse that ran away with her during a ride at Cambridge.

LADY LAZARUS[1]

I have done it again.
One year in every ten
I manage it—

A sort of walking miracle, my skin
Bright as a Nazi lampshade,[2]
My right foot

A paperweight,
My face a featureless, fine
Jew linen.

Peel off the napkin
O my enemy.
Do I terrify?—

The nose, the eye pits, the full set of teeth?
The sour breath
Will vanish in a day.

Soon, soon the flesh
The grave cave ate will be
At home on me

And I a smiling woman.
I am only thirty.
And like the cat I have nine times to die.

This is Number Three.
What a trash
To annihilate each decade.

What a million filaments.
The peanut-crunching crowd
Shoves in to see

Them unwrap me hand and foot—
The big strip tease.
Gentlemen, ladies

These are my hands
My knees.
I may be skin and bone,

Nevertheless, I am the same, identical woman.
The first time it happened I was ten.
It was an accident.

The second time I meant
To last it out and not come back at all.
I rocked shut

As a seashell.
They had to call and call
And pick the worms off me like sticky pearls.

Dying
Is an art, like everything else.
I do it exceptionally well.

I do it so it feels like hell.
I do it so it feels real.
I guess you could say I've a call.

It's easy enough to do it in a cell.
It's easy enough to do it and stay put.
It's the theatrical

Comeback in broad day
To the same place, the same face, the same brute
Amused shout:

'A miracle!'
That knocks me out.
There is a charge

For the eyeing of my scars, there is a charge
For the hearing of my heart—
It really goes.

And there is a charge, a very large charge
For a word or a touch
Or a bit of blood

Or a piece of my hair or my clothes.
So, so, Herr Doktor.
So, Herr Enemy.

I am your opus,
I am your valuable,
The pure gold baby

That melts to a shriek.
I turn and burn.
Do not think I underestimate your great concern.

Ash, ash—
You poke and stir.
Flesh, bone, there is nothing there—

A cake of soap,
A wedding ring,
A gold filling.[3]

Herr God, Herr Lucifer
Beware
Beware.

Out of the ash
I rise with my red hair
And I eat men like air.

Fall 1962

    [1]*Lady Lazarus* Lazarus was a man Jesus raised from the dead. [2]In one concentration camp an administrator had lampshades made from the skins of men with interesting tattoos. [3]The dead were burned in furnaces. Their wedding rings and tooth fillings were saved for the gold in them. In some places the bodies were made into soap.

DADDY

You do not do, you do not do
Any more, black shoe
In which I have lived like a foot
For thirty years, poor and white,
Barely daring to breathe or Achoo.

Daddy, I have had to kill you.
You died before I had time—
Marble-heavy, a bag full of God,
Ghastly statue with one grey toe
Big as a Frisco seal

And a head in the freakish Atlantic
Where it pours bean green over blue
In the waters off beautiful Nauset.
I used to pray to recover you.
Ach, du.

In the German tongue, in the Polish town
Scraped flat by the roller
Of wars, wars, wars.
But the name of the town is common.
My Polack friend

Says there are a dozen or two.
So I never could tell where you
Put your foot, your root,
I never could talk to you.
The tongue stuck in my jaw.

It stuck in a barb wire snare.
Ich, ich, ich, ich,
I could hardly speak.
I thought every German was you.
And the language obscene

An engine, an engine
Chuffing me off like a Jew.
A Jew to Dachau, Auschwitz, Belsen.[1]
I began to talk like a Jew.
I think I may well be a Jew.

The snows of the Tyrol, the clear beer of Vienna
Are not very pure or true.
With my gypsy ancestress and my weird luck
And my Taroc pack and my Taroc pack
I may be a bit of a Jew.

I have always been scared of *you*,
With your Luftwaffe,[2] your gobbledygoo.
And your neat moustache
And your Aryan eye, bright blue.
Panzer-man, panzer-man,[3] O You—

Not God but a swastika
So black no sky could squeak through.
Every woman adores a Fascist,
The boot in the face, the brute
Brute heart of a brute like you.

You stand at the blackboard, daddy,
In the picture I have of you,
A cleft in your chin instead of your foot
But no less a devil for that, no not
Any less the black man who

Bit my pretty red heart in two.
I was ten when they buried you.
At twenty I tried to die
And get back, back, back to you.
I thought even the bones would do.

But they pulled me out of the sack,
And they stuck me together with glue.

And then I knew what to do.
I made a model of you,
A man in black with a Meinkampf look[4]

And a love of the rack and the screw.
And I said I do, I do.
So daddy, I'm finally through.
The black telephone's off at the root,
The voices just can't worm through.

If I've killed one man, I've killed two—
The vampire who said he was you
And drank my blood for a year,
Seven years, if you want to know.
Daddy, you can lie back now.

There's a stake in your fat black heart[5]
And the villagers never liked you.
They are dancing and stamping on you.
They always *knew* it was you.
Daddy, daddy, you bastard, I'm through.

October-November 1962

[1]*Dachau, Auschwitz, Belsen* locations of concentration camps for Jews. [2]*Luftwaffe* (German) the German air force (*Luft waffe* means "air weapon"). [3]In the Nazi mythology of racism, Aryans were the master race—tall, blonde, Nordic types with blue eyes. A panzer-man was a tank driver (*panzer* means "armor"). [4]*Meinkampf* (German) "my battle," the title of Adolf Hitler's book setting forth his theories of racism. [5]In folklore a vampire is a corpse come to life again that leaves its grave at night to feed on human blood. It can be "killed" by a stake driven through its heart.

EDGE

The woman is perfected.
Her dead

Body wears the smile of accomplishment,
The illusion of a Greek necessity

Flows in the scrolls of her toga,
Her bare

Feet seem to be saying:
We have come so far, it is over.

Each dead child coiled, a white serpent,
One at each little

Pitcher of milk, now empty.
She has folded

Them back into her body as petals
Of a rose close when the garden

Stiffens and odours bleed
From the sweet, deep throats of the night flower.

The moon has nothing to be sad about,
Staring from her hood of bone.

She is used to this sort of thing.
Her blacks crackle and drag.

February 1963

WORDS

Axes
After whose stroke the wood rings,
And the echoes!
Echoes travelling
Off from the centre like horses.

The sap
Wells like tears, like the
Water striving
To re-establish its mirror
Over the rock

That drops and turns,
A white skull,
Eaten by weedy greens.
Years later I
Encounter them on the road—

Words dry and riderless,
The indefatigable hoof-taps.
While
From the bottom of the pool, fixed stars
Govern a life.

February 1963

SAM COOKE

Sam Cooke (born in Clarksdale, Mississippi) first sang in the choir of his father's church. He had earned a reputation as a gospel singer before he recorded his first popular song, "You Send Me" (1953), a record that sold more than two million copies. Cooke was about thirty years old in 1964 when he died in Los Angeles of gunshot wounds.

The first version of "A Change Is Gonna Come" comes from *The Best of Sam Cooke,* Vol. 2 (1965); the second, as sung by Otis Redding, comes from *Otis Blue—Otis Redding Sings Soul* (VOLT LP 412, 1965).

A CHANGE IS GONNA COME

I was born by the river
In a little tent.
And just like the river
I been runnin' ever since.
    It's been a long, a long time comin'
    But I know a change gon' come,
    O yes it will.

It's been too hard livin'
But I'm afraid to die.
I don't know what's up there
Beyond the sky.
    It's been a long, a long time comin'
    But I know a change gon' come,
    O yes it will.

    Then I go to my brother,
    And I say, "Brother, help me, please."
    But he winds up knockin' me
    Back down on my knees.

There been times that I thought
Lord it's bad to bear it alone,
But now I think I'm able to carry on.
    It's been a long, a long time comin'
    But I know a change gon' come,
    O yes it will.

CHANGE GONNA COME[1]
(OTIS REDDING)

I was born by the river
In this little old tent.
Just like this river
I been runnin' ever since.
>It's been a long, long, long time comin'
>But I know, but I know a change has got to come.
>O yes it is.

It's been too hard livin'
And I'm afraid to die.
I don't know what's up there
Beyond the clouds.
>It's been a long, long, long time comin'
>But I know, but I know a change has got to come.
>O yes it is.

>There's a time I will go to my brother,
>I've asked my brother, "Will you help me, please?"
>He turned me down and then I asked my dear mother,
>I said, "Mother," I said "Mother, I'm down on my knees."

It's been a time that I thought
It's too late to bear it alone,
Somehow I thought I was still able
To try to carry on.
>It's been a long, long, long time comin'
>But I know a change is gonna come.
>O yes it is.

---

[1] The two versions of this song—one by Sam Cooke, the other by Otis Redding—illustrate some important characteristics of singers, songs, and poetry. Many of the popular singers are poets too, although they limit themselves to making small changes in songs they have chosen to perform themselves. Otis Redding's version is partly an original song (and poem)—for example, when he adds a visit to his "dear mother." Redding of course may have heard some of the words differently from the way Cooke recorded them. Poets consciously borrow themes, images, or metaphors from other poets and then work changes upon the material they have borrowed, perhaps because they understand an idea in a different way or perhaps because they feel they can make the old material say something new. The custom of borrowing from another's work and carrying it on in a new form is what makes traditional arts of song and poetry. Part of the value of both is that they can register the slow or rapid changes of culture, feeling, and style.

IMAMU AMIRI BARAKA

Imamu Amiri Baraka, formerly LeRoi Jones (born 1934 in Newark, New Jersey), is a brilliant playwright *(The Toilet, Dutchman, The Slave, Slave Ship, Four Revolutionary Black Plays,* and *Jello).* He was arrested during the 1967 riots in Newark. He lives in Newark with his second wife Ameena and three children. Baraka says of his early poetry that it was filled with a sense of despair and a preoccupation with his own death, because he was "caught up in the deathurge of this twisted society."* Since 1966 Baraka's work has been "less passive . . . less uselessly 'literary' " and has become "self-consciously spiritual, and stronger," because it is in touch with the "whole race connected in its darkness." The poems are from *The Dead Lecturer* (1964) and *Black Magic Poetry 1961-1967* (1969).

I SUBSTITUTE FOR THE DEAD LECTURER

What is most precious, because
it is lost. What is lost,
because it is most
precious.

They have turned, and say that I am dying. That
I have thrown
my life
away. They
have left me alone, where
there is no one, nothing
save who I am. Not a note
nor a word.

---

*This and the following quotations are from a preface to *Black Magic, Sabotage* (1961-1963), *Target Practice Study* (1963-1965), and *Black Art* (1965-1966) (Indianapolis: Bobbs-Merrill).

                Cold air batters
the poor (and their minds
turn open
like sores). What kindness
What wealth
can I offer? Except
what is, for me,
ugliest. What is
for me, shadows, shrieking
phantoms. Except
they have need
of life. Flesh
at least,
            should be theirs.

The Lord has saved me
to do this. The Lord
has made me strong. I
am as I must have
myself. Against all
thought, all music, all
my soft loves.

                For all these wan roads
I am pushed to follow, are
my own conceit. A simple muttering
elegance, slipped in my head
pressed on my soul, is my heart's
worth. And I am frightened
that the flame of my sickness
will burn off my face. And leave
the bones, my stewed black skull,
an empty cage of failure.

A POEM SOME PEOPLE WILL HAVE TO UNDERSTAND

Dull unwashed windows of eyes
and buildings of industry. What
industry do I practice? A slick
colored boy, 12 miles from his
home. I practice no industry.

I am no longer a credit
to my race. I read a little,
scratch against silence slow spring
afternoons.
               I had thought, before, some years ago
that I'd come to the end of my life.
               Watercolor ego. Without the preciseness
a violent man could propose.
               But the wheel, and the wheels,
wont let us alone. All the fantasy
               and justice, and dry charcoal winters
All the pitifully intelligent citizens
               I've forced myself to love.

               We have awaited the coming of a natural
               phenomenon. Mystics and romantics, knowledgeable
               workers
               of the land.

               But none has come.
               (Repeat)
                             but none has come.

Will the machinegunners please step forward?

RED LIGHT

The only thing we know is the thing
we turn out to be, I don't care what
you think, it's true, now you think
your way out of this

POEM FOR HALFWHITE COLLEGE STUDENTS

Who are you, listening to me, who are you
listening to yourself? Are you white or
black, or does that have anything to do
with it? Can you pop your fingers to no
music, except those wild monkies go on
in your head, can you jerk, to no melody,
except finger poppers get it together
when you turn from starchecking to checking

yourself. How do you sound, your words, are they
yours? The ghost you see in the mirror, is it really
you, can you swear you are not an imitation greyboy,
can you look right next to you in that chair, and swear,
that the sister you have your hand on is not really
so full of Elizabeth Taylor, Richard Burton is
coming out of her ears. You may even have to be Richard
with a white shirt and face, and four million negroes
think you cute, you may have to be Elizabeth Taylor, old lady,
if you want to sit up in your crazy spot dreaming about dresses,
and the sway of certain porters' hips. Check yourself, learn who it is
speaking, when you make some ultrasophisticated point, check yourself,
when you find yourself gesturing like Steve McQueen, check it out, ask
in your black heart who it is you are, and is that image black or white,

you might be surprised right out the window, whistling dixie on the
    way in.

LOKU

Hold me she
told me I
did.

AMERICAN ECSTASY[1]

"Loss of Life or Both Feet or Both Hands or Both Eyes
    .... The Principal Sum
Loss of One Hand and One Foot
    .... The Principal Sum
Loss of One Hand and One Eye or One Foot and One Eye
    .... The Principal Sum
Loss of One Hand or One Foot
    .... One half The PRINCIPAL Sum
Loss of One Eye
    .... One fourth The Principal Sum"

[1] a portion of an insurance policy and an example of "found" poetry, which is an utterance that has a naive poetic quality but which the author did not intend as poetry.

CHUCK BERRY

Chuck Berry was born in St. Louis in 1936. He worked as a hair stylist before he became a singer. He lives at Berry Park, a motel and nightclub development of which he is proprietor, near Wentsville, Missouri.

"Too Much Monkey Business" and "Roll Over, Beethoven" were recorded in 1956 on the Chess label. The Beatles revived "Roll Over, Beethoven" in 1964. Both songs appear on *Chuck Berry's Greatest Hits,* Chess LP-1485.

TOO MUCH MONKEY BUSINESS*

Runnin' to and fro
Hard workin' at the mill,
Never fail
In the mail
Here come
A rotten bill.
Too much monkey business,
Too much monkey business,
Too much monkey business,
For me to be involved in.

See 'em talkin' to me
Tryin' to run me up a creek,
Say, "You can buy it,
Go on try it,
You can pay me
Next week."
Too much monkey business,
Too much monkey business,
Too much monkey business,
For me to be involved in.

Blonde hair, good lookin'
Tryin' to get me hooked.
Want me to marry,
Get a job,

---

* © copyright 1956 Arc Music Corp. Used with permission of the Publisher. All rights reserved.

Get a home,
Write a book.
Too much monkey business,
Too much monkey business,
Too much monkey business,
For me to be involved in.

Same thing every day
Gettin' up, goin' to school.
No need
Of me complainin'
My objection's
Overruled.
Too much monkey business,
Too much monkey business,
Too much monkey business,
For me to be involved in.

Pay phone, sumthin' wrong,
Dime gone, will mail.
Oughta sue
The operator
For tellin' me
A tale.
Too much monkey business,
Too much monkey business,
Too much monkey business,
For me to be involved in.

I been to Yokahama
Been fightin' in the war,
Army bunk,
Army child,
Army clothes,
Army car.
Too much monkey business,
Too much monkey business,
Too much monkey business,
For me to be involved in.

Workin' in the fillin' station,
Too many tasks.
Wipe the windows,

Check the tires,
Check the oil,
A dollar gas.
I don't want your botheration.
Get away, leave me.
Too much monkey business for me.

ROLL OVER, BEETHOVEN*

Well, I'm gonna write a letter
Gonna mail it to my local deejay.
Yeah, there's a jumpin' little record
I want my jockey to play.
Roll over, Beethoven,
I gotta hear it again today.

You know my temperature risin'
The juke box blowin' a fuse.
My heart beatin' rhythm
And my soul keep a-singin' the blues.
Roll over, Beethoven,
And tell Tchaikovsky the news.

I got the rockin' pneumonia,
I need a shot of rhythm and blues.
I caught the rollin' off a writer
Sittin' down at a rhythm review.
Roll over, Beethoven,
They're rockin' in two by two.

Well, if you feel it and like it,
Go get your lover,
Then reel and rock it,
Roll it over.
Then move on up
Just a trifle further,
Then reel and rock
With one another.
Roll over, Beethoven,
And dig these rhythm and blues.

* © copyright 1956 Arc Music Corp. Used with permission of the Publisher. All rights reserved.

Well, early in the morning—I'm givin' you my warning—
Don't you step on my blue suede shoes.
Hey diddle, diddle, I'm a-playin' my fiddle,
Ain't got nothin' to lose.
Roll over, Beethoven,
And tell Tchaikovsky the news.

You know she wiggle like a glow worm
Dance like a spinnin' top.
She got a crazy partner,
You oughta see him reel and rock.
Long as she got a dime,
The music won't never stop.

Roll over, Beethoven,
Roll over, Beethoven,
Roll over, Beethoven,
Roll over, Beethoven,
Roll over, Beethoven,
Dig these rhythm and blues.

ZEL SANDERS AND LONA STEVENS
(PSEUDONYM FOR LONA SPECTOR)

"Sally, Go 'Round the Roses" was a hit song of 1963, written for the Jaynettes, who performed on the Tuff label.

SALLY, GO 'ROUND THE ROSES*

Sally, go 'round the roses.
Sally, go 'round the roses.
Sally, go 'round the roses.
Sally, go 'round the pretty roses.

The roses, they can't hurt you.
No, the roses, they can't hurt you.
The roses, they can't hurt you.
No, the roses, they can't hurt you.

Sally, doncha go, doncha go downtown.
Sally, doncha go, doncha go downtown.
The saddest thing in this whole wide world
Is to see your baby with another girl.

Sally, go 'round the roses.
Sally, go 'round the roses.
Sally, go 'round the roses.
Sally, go 'round the pretty roses.

They won't tell your secrets.
They won't tell your secrets.
They won't tell your secrets.
No, the roses won't tell your secrets.

Sally, baby, cry; let your hair hang down.
Sally, baby, cry; let your hair hang down.
Sit and cry where the roses grow,
You can sit and cry and not a soul will know.

Sally, go 'round the roses.

* from the song *Sally Go 'Round the Roses*. Copyright © 1963, Winlyn Music Inc. Used by permission. All rights reserved.

SONIA SANCHEZ

Sonia Sanchez was born in Birmingham, Alabama, in 1935. She went to school at Hunter College (New York City), and she has taught in New York City and at San Francisco State College. She writes plays as well as poems. The poems are from *Homecoming* (1969).

MALCOLM

do not speak to me of martyrdom
of men who die to be remembered
on some parish day.
i don't believe in dying
though i too shall die
and violets like castanets
will echo me.

yet this man
this dreamer,
thick-lipped with words
will never speak again
and in each winter
when the cold air cracks
with frost, i'll breathe
his breath and mourn
my gun-filled nights.
he was the sun that tagged
the western sky and
melted tiger-scholars
while they searched for stripes.
he said, "fuck you white
man. we have been
curled too long, nothing
is sacred now. not your
white faces nor any
land that separates
until some voices
squat with spasms."

do not speak to me of living.
life is obscene with crowds
of white on black.
death is my pulse.
what might have been
is not for him/or me
but what could have been
floods the womb until i drown.

POEM
(FOR DCS 8TH GRADERS—1966-67)

look at me 8th
grade
     i am black
beautiful. i have a
man who looks at
my face and smiles.
on my face
are black warriors
riding in ships
of slavery;
       on my face
               is malcolm
                     spitting his metal seeds
on a country of sheep;
on my face
     are young eyes
breathing in black crusts.
             look at us
8th grade
     we are black
beautiful and our black
ness sings out
         while america wanders
dumb with her wet bowels.

LUCILLE CLIFTON

Lucille Clifton (1936, Depew, New York) attended State University of New York—Fredonia College (Fredonia, New York). She lives in Baltimore with her husband and six children. The poems come from *Good Times* (1969).

IN THE INNER CITY

in the inner city
or
like we call it
home
we think a lot about uptown
and the silent nights
and the houses straight as
dead men
and the pastel lights
and we hang on to our no place
happy to be alive
and in the inner city
or
like we call it
home

GOOD TIMES

My Daddy has paid the rent
and the insurance man is gone
and the lights is back on
and my uncle Brud has hit
for one dollar straight
and they is good times
good times
good times

My Mama has made bread
and Grampaw has come
and everybody is drunk
and dancing in the kitchen
and singing in the kitchen
oh these is good times
good times
good times

oh children think about the
good times

CA'LINE'S PRAYER

I have got old
in a desert country
I am dry
and black as drought
don't make water
only acid
even dogs won't drink

Remember me from Wydah
Remember the child
running across Dahomey
black as ripe papaya
juicy as sweet berries
and set me in the rivers of your glory

Ye Ma Jah

FOR DELAWD

people say they have a hard time
understanding how I
go on about my business
playing my Ray Charles
hollering at the kids—
seem like my Afro
cut off in some old image

would show I got a long memory
and I come from a line
of black and going on women
who got used to making it through murdered sons
and who grief kept on pushing
who fried chicken
ironed
swept off the back steps
who grief kept
for their still alive sons
for their sons coming
for their sons gone
just pushing

ADMONITIONS

boys
i don't promise you nothing
but this
what you pawn
i will redeem
what you steal
i will conceal
my private silence to
your public guilt
is all i got

girls
first time a white man
opens his fly
like a good thing
we'll just laugh
laugh real loud my
black women

children
when they ask you
why is your mama so funny
say she is a poet
she don't have no sense

DIANE WAKOSKI

Diane Wakoski has worked as a bookstore clerk and a teacher in junior high school. She has taught at the New School for Social Research in New York City. She is a past editor of *Dream Sheet* and *Software*. She was born in 1937 in Whittier, California, and went to school at the University of California, Berkeley. "Reaching Out with the Hands of the Sun" comes from *The Magellanic Clouds* (1970).

REACHING OUT WITH THE HANDS OF THE SUN

> *And thereupon*
> *That beautiful mild woman for whose sake*
> *There's many a one shall find out all heartache*
> *On finding that her voice is sweet & low*
> *Replied: 'To be born woman is to know—*
> *Although they do not talk of it at school—*
> *That we must labour to be beautiful.'*
>
> "Adam's Curse," W. B. Yeats

Atun-Re
the sun disk
whose rays end in hands
shines above us in New York
California
Egypt
sometimes even Alaska.
Walking across the desert,
he puts his scorching hands over our eyes
and turns vision into sounds,
waves
as the ocean,
drawing the pupils away from rattlesnakes & blurring
the hawks
that sail so unconcerned with heat
above our heads;
when we ride across the snow
and shaggy trees of Alaska

the sun's many hands
rub thick bear skins & tallow against the apples of our faces;
when we float down the river
without barks of gold or flutes or beautiful boys in the heavy
linen sails,
the sun's hands reach into the Nile
and pull out a glimmering eel
or a water lily,
holding it against the banks,
motioning for us to expect life anywhere,
even though it's not at once seen;
the hands coming from the rays of that disk
hold oranges, dates, figs, nuts
all those sweetmeats
that give a woman fat thighs
and a puffy face.

What am I to believe in this world?
The whirling sun disk
that speeds years away
puts out such rays with hands attached to each
that fling me one day against
the rough edges of mountains,
one day caress me, push me against the long mustaches I love;
my face varies from plain to dignified;
my figure from straight to plump;
my eyes from bright to small & sad;
my mouth, always a straight line—as if crossing a "t"
and I see the world change around me;
only one thing never changes.

Men remember,
love,
cherish,
beautiful women,
    as I've said,
      like April snow
like silk that rustles in a fragrant chest,
like a machine dripping with oil and running smoothly.

I am pooh-poohed
every time I say it.
    "a woman of your intelligence,"
      etc., etc.,

believing
such a superficial thing. "Only the
foolish
misguided,
the men with no balls,
or the ones that don't really matter,"
love a woman for her beauty
her physical self.
But I know different.
I've ruled;
I've walked with the mask of a falcon,
perhaps Horus
over my head,
walked everywhere, stiff & disguised,
walked in stone watching
the life around me,
the loving,
and not loving,
without sounds to interrupt or change history.
I've watched and know
that even the poets
whose blood is most filled with sun's light
and whose hands are wet
coming out of the rays of the moon,
love beautiful women,
writhe, turn,
upset their lives, leave their good wives,
when one walks by.
And we,
with fat thighs,
or small breasts,
or thin delicate hair,
pale faces,
small eyes,
with only our elegant, small-wristed hands
to defend us
trying to catch one of the hands
on a ray from the sun,
loving our men faithfully
and with hope;
surely we deserve something more than platitudes.

We are the ones who know
     beauty is only skin deep.
But we also know
we would trade every ruby
stuffing and jamming our wealthy opulent hearts;
would trade every silver whistle
that alerts our brain,
keeps us sensitive and graceful to the world;
would trade every
miracle
inside our plain & ugly blood factories,
these bodies that never
serve us well,
for some beauty
they could recognize;
that would make the men stop
turn their heads,
twist their minds & lives around
for us/
for those of us who love them
and who never stop.
Whose hands are always radiating
out
ready to touch
the men
with fire
direct from the solar disk
who
brood
are dark often
with hands that come from the
unseen side
of the moon.

ISHMAEL REED

Ishmael Reed was born in Chattanooga, Tennessee, in 1938. He attended the University of Buffalo. Mr. Reed is author of *The Free-Lance Pallbearers* (1967), *Yellow Back Radio Broke-Down* (1969), and *Mumbo Jumbo* (1972), all novels published by Doubleday. He is editor of *19 Necromancers from Now*. His first collection of poems by an American publisher, *Conjure,* will be published in October 1972 by The University of Massachusetts Press. "I Am a Cowboy in the Boat of Ra" is from *Catechism of d Neoamerican Hoodoo Church* (1970).

I AM A COWBOY IN THE BOAT OF RA

"The devil must be forced to reveal any such
physical evil (potions, charms, fetishes, etc.) still
outside the body and these must be burned."
—Rituale Romanum, *published 1947, endorsed*
by the coat of arms and introduction letter from
Francis Cardinal Spellman

I am a cowboy in the boat of Ra,[1]
sidewinders in the saloons of fools
bit my forehead   like   O
the untrustworthiness of Egyptologists
who do not know their trips. Who was that
dog-faced man? they asked, the day I rode
from town.

School marms with halitosis cannot see
the Nefertiti[2] fake chipped on the run by slick
germans, the hawk behind Sonny Rollins'[3] head or
the ritual beard of his axe; a longhorn winding
its bells thru the Field of Reeds.

I am a cowboy in the boat of Ra. I bedded
down with Isis,[4] Lady of the Boogaloo, dove
down deep in her horny, stuck up her Wells-Far-ago
in daring midday get away. "Start grabbing the
blue," i said from top of my double crown.

I am a cowboy in the boat of Ra. Ezzard Charles[5]
of the Chisholm Trail. Took up the bass but they
blew off my thumb. Alchemist in ringmanship but a
sucker for the right cross.

I am a cowboy in the boat of Ra. Vamoosed from
the temple i bide my time. The price on the wanted
poster was a-going down, outlaw alias copped my stance
and moody greenhorns were making me dance; while my mouth's
shooting iron got its chambers jammed.

I am a cowboy in the boat of Ra. Boning-up in
the ol West i bide my time. You should see
me pick off these tin cans whippersnappers. I
write the motown long plays for the comeback of
Osiris.[6] Make them up when stars stare at sleeping
steer out here near the campfire. Women arrive
on the backs of goats and throw themselves on
my Bowie.

I am a cowboy in the boat of Ra. Lord of the lash,
the Loup Garou Kid. Half breed son of Pisces and
Aquarius. I hold the souls of men in my pot. I do
the dirty boogie with scorpions. I make the bulls
keep still and was the first swinger to grape the taste.

I am a cowboy in his boat. Pope Joan of the
Ptah Ra. C/mere a minute willya doll?
Be a good girl and
Bring me my Buffalo horn of black powder
Bring me my headdress of black feathers
Bring me my bones of Ju-Ju snake
Go get my eyelids of red paint.
Hand me my shadow

I'm going into town after Set

I am a cowboy in the boat of Ra

look out Set   here i come Set
to get Set   to sunset Set
to unseat Set   to Set down Set

usurper of the Royal couch
imposter RAdio of Moses' bush
party pooper O hater of dance
vampire outlaw of the milky way

¹*Ra* Egyptian sun god. ²*Nefertiti* queen of Egypt (14th Century B.C.) ³*Sonny Rollins* jazz saxophone player. ⁴*Isis* Egyptian nature goddess and universal mother. Wife of Osiris. ⁵*Ezzard Charles* prizefighter. ⁶*Osiris* god of the underworld, associated with fertility and immortality.

CHARLES SIMIC

Charles Simic (1938, Belgrade, Yugoslavia) has translated French, Russian, and Yugoslav poetry. He studied at New York University, and now teaches in the English department of California State College, Hayward. The poems are from *Dismantling the Silence* (1971).

MY SHOES

Shoes, secret face of my inner life:
Two gaping toothless mouths,
Two partly decomposed animal skins
Smelling of mice-nests.

My brother and sister who died at birth
Continuing their existence in you,
Guiding my life
Toward their incomprehensible innocence.

What use are books to me
When in you it is possible to read
The Gospel of my life on earth
And still beyond, of things to come?

I want to proclaim the religion
I have devised for your perfect humility
And the strange church I am building
With you as the altar.

Ascetic and maternal, you endure:
Kin to oxen, to Saints, to condemned men,
With your mute patience, forming
The only true likeness of myself.

STONE

Go inside a stone
That would be my way.
Let somebody else become a dove

Or gnash with a tiger's tooth.
I am happy to be a stone.

From the outside the stone is a riddle:
No one knows how to answer it.
Yet within, it must be cool and quiet
Even though a cow steps on it full weight,
Even though a child throws it in a river;
The stone sinks, slow, unperturbed
To the river bottom
Where the fishes come to knock on it
And listen.

I have seen sparks fly out
When two stones are rubbed,
So perhaps it is not dark inside after all;
Perhaps there is a moon shining
From somewhere, as though behind a hill—
Just enough light to make out
The strange writings, the star-charts
On the inner walls.

POEM WITHOUT A TITLE

I say to the lead
Why did you let yourself
Be cast into a bullet?
Have you forgotten the alchemists?
Have you given up hope
Of turning into gold?

Nobody answers.
Lead. Bullet. With names
Such as these
The sleep is deep and long.

STONE INSIDE A STONE

1

They will not turn into seed.
On the border of nothing and nothing.

Fossils of the wind.
But what wind?

You can't step twice in the same river—
With a stone you can take your sweet time.

Going to pick a flower in its heart
Is like taking a live chicken out of a bottle.

My stones will not sing the song yours are singing.

They say: everything is so simple. Touch it.
You awake in one, fall asleep in another.

Who, while the night is still deep, awakes the roosters?
A stone among us is taking notes.

The opposite has ceased to be imaginary.
There are two of us now but o what solitude.

2

Touch again. You've touched a lightning.
The thunder is still to come.

Once in my hand
The fingers speak to it in its own language.

Stone, you come from a long line of fire-thieves.
I answered your questions
Until your hardness entered my voice.
Now they can carve whatever tool they please.

This is bread never-sown, never-reaped.

Two of them hang in death's testicles.

Strength that wishes to contract
Until it resembles itself more fully.

I hear the steps of the stone.
I lift them with my tongue
To keep myself in shape
For an unknown time.

FLORENCE ELON

Florence Elon was born in New York City in 1939. She has attended the City University of New York, the Free University of Berlin, Stanford University (as a Fellow in the creative writing program), and the University of California at Berkeley. Her collection of poems, *Clock Ticks,* won first prize in the 1970 Camden Festival in England. She lives in San Francisco with her husband, Alex Zwerdling. The poems were taken from two periodicals, *The Canadian Forum* (September 1965) and *The Massachusetts Review* (1966). "Berlin: the Ruined Countess" also was read on the BBC Third Program in London, England.

VISITING HOURS

Daughters he used to dress,
whose skinny legs he pushed to run
on Orchard Street
and bitten nails he forced to grow,
whose meat he bought and hides he tanned
sit on his bed

and cramp his feet.
Dressed up in furs like the minks
he used to skin, and underneath,
in tailored suits
they hand him daisies, stems clipped short.
Their hands wear polished, sharpened nails.

Smiling at his yellowing gown,
the brown spot on his nail that won't
grow out in time, his mumbled prayers
they can no longer say, their mouths
whose wails he used to kiss away
have now forgotten how to speak.

BERLIN: THE RUINED COUNTESS

Down Kurfürstendamm, tapping her cane,
the Countess von der Kranzenberg sweeps
her frayed hems back and forth
while cats and children scatter.

Now swerving round the corner
she unlocks the oak door,
scorched and peeling, of her "villa,"
stoops to brush mud tracks from the threshold.

Chin cocked back, she taps along the hall,
pausing at our keyhole
to see sheer nylons
dripping from her chandeliers.

And though she swears twenty-six Cossacks
enjoyed her in three weeks,
at night I catch her,
knees shaking, hunched by our door.

Next morning, in the kitchen,
poking a cauldron
of embroidered undershirts, she complains
about bed creaks after midnight.

Before lunch, she pinches bits
of liver from my pan, hangs them up
on pegs in the closet,
but forgets them among her aging wursts;

days later, I trace the green smells.
Upstairs, on a faded coverlet,
she spreads gilt edged medals,
carved serpent handles of sabers,

and curling blacks and whites of the Count
with his tulip hipped wife, to whose bed,
neighbors whisper, she, lace capped,
may have carried the last chamberpot.

FLORENCE ELON

JAMES WELCH

James Welch (1940, Browning, Montana) is a Blackfoot Indian who grew up in the Northwest and in Minnesota, who was graduated from high school in Minneapolis and attended the University of Minnesota, Northern Montana College, and the University of Montana. He now lives and writes in Upper Rattlesnake near Missoula, Montana. The poems come from *Riding the Earthboy 40* (1971), and *Hearse* (No. 14, 1970).

GETTING THINGS STRAIGHT

Is the sun the same drab gold?
The hawk—is he still rising, circling,
falling above the field? And the rolling day,
it will never stop? It means nothing?
Will it end the way history ended when
the last giant climbed Heart Butte, had his vision,
came back to town and drank himself
sick? The hawk has spotted a mouse.
Wheeling, falling, stumbling to a stop,
he watches the snake ribbon quickly
under a rock. What does it mean?
He flashes his wings to the sun, bobs
twice and lifts, screaming
off the ground. Does it mean this to him:
the mouse, a snake, the dozen angry days
still rolling since his last good feed?
Who offers him a friendly meal?
Am I strangling in his grip?
Is he my vision?

HARLEM, MONTANA:
JUST OFF THE RESERVATION

We need no runners here. Booze is law
and all the Indians drink in the best tavern.
Money is free if you're poor enough.
Disgusted, busted whites are running
for office in this town. The constable,
a local farmer, plants the jail with wild
raven-haired stiffs who beg just one more drink.
One drunk, a former Methodist, becomes a saint
in the Indian church, bugs the plaster man
on the cross with snakes. If his knuckles broke,
he'd see those women wail the graves goodbye.

Goodbye, goodbye, Harlem on the rocks,
so bigoted, you forget the latest joke,
so lonely, you'd welcome a battalion of Turks
to rule your women. What you don't know,
what you will never know or want to learn—
Turks aren't white. Turks are olive, unwelcome
alive in any town. Turks would use
your one dingy park to declare a need for loot.
Turks say bring it, step quickly, lay down and dead.

Here we are when men were nice. This photo, hung
in the New England Hotel lobby, shows them nicer
than pie, agreeable to the warring bands of redskins
who demanded protection money for the price of food.
Now, only Hutterites out north are nice. We hate
them. They are tough and their crops are always good.
We accuse them of idiocy and believe their belief all wrong.

Harlem, your hotel is overnamed, your children
are raggedy-assed but you go on, survive
the bad food from the two cafes and peddle
your hate for the wild who bring you money.
When you die, if you die, will you remember
the three young bucks who shot the grocery up,
locked themselves in and cried for days, we're rich,
help us, oh God, we're rich.

GRACE SLICK

Grace Slick was born (1940) and raised in Palo Alto, California. Her father is an investment banker in San Francisco. She married and later divorced Jerry Slick, a filmmaker. In 1965 she was singing with a group in San Francisco called The Great Society; Signe Andersen was the female vocalist with The Jefferson Airplane. When Signe Andersen left The Airplane, Grace Slick took her place. She now lives in Bolinas, California, with Paul Kantner of The Airplane and their daughter. "White Rabbit" appears on the album *Surrealistic Pillow* (1967).

WHITE RABBIT

One pill makes you larger
And one pill makes you small,
And the ones that mother gives you
Don't do anything at all,
Go ask Alice
When she's ten feet tall

And if you go chasing rabbits
And you know you're going to fall,
Tell them all who got silken colored hair[1]
Has given you the call,
Call Alice
When she was just small.

When the men[2] on the chessboard get up and tell you where to go
And you've just had some kind of mushroom
And your mind is moving low,
Go ask Alice
I think she'll know.

When the logic[3] and proportion
Have fallen so I'll be dead,[4]
And the White Knight is talking backwards
And the Red Queens are ahead,[5]
Remember what the dormouse said;
"Heed your head.[6]
Heed your head."

[1]"Tell 'em a hookah smoking caterpillar." [2]"When men." [3]"When logic." [4]"Have fallen sloppy dead." [5]"And the Red Queen's lost her head." [6]"Feed your head, Feed your head, Feed your head." (These are variants from sheet music copy (copyright 1966), Copperpenny Music Publishing Company as reprinted in (ed.) Richard Goldstein, *The Poetry of Rock* (New York: Bantam, 1969).)

OTIS REDDING

Otis Redding (1941, Dawson, Georgia) grew up in Macon, Georgia, the home town of Little Richard. He made his first recording in 1962. Earlier he was a vocalist with Johnny Jenkins and the Pinetoppers. Five years later he performed at the Monterey Pop Festival. He died in 1967 in Lake Pomona, Wisconsin, when his private plane crashed after a concert in Madison, Wisconsin. "Dock of the Bay," written in collaboration with Steve Cropper, comes from *The Dock of the Bay* Volt S-419 (1968).

THE DOCK OF THE BAY

Sittin' in the morning sun,
I'll be sittin' when the evenin' come,
Watchin' the ships roll in,
Then I watch 'em roll away again,
Yeah I'm sittin' on the dock of a bay
Watchin' the tide roll away,
Sittin' on a dock of a bay, wastin' time.

I left my home in Georgia,
Headed for the Frisco bay,
'Cause I've had nothing to live for
And look like nothing's gonna come my way,
So I'm just gonna sit on the dock of a bay
Watchin' the tide roll away,
Sittin' on a dock of a bay, wastin' time.

    Look like nothing's gonna change,
    Everything still remains the same,
    I can't do what ten people tell me to do,
    So I guess I'll remain the same.

Sittin' here restin' my bones
And this loneliness won't leave me alone,
Two thousand miles I roam
Just to make this dock my home,
Now I'm just gon' sit at the dock of a bay
Watchin' the tide roll away,
Sittin' on a dock of a bay, wastin' time.

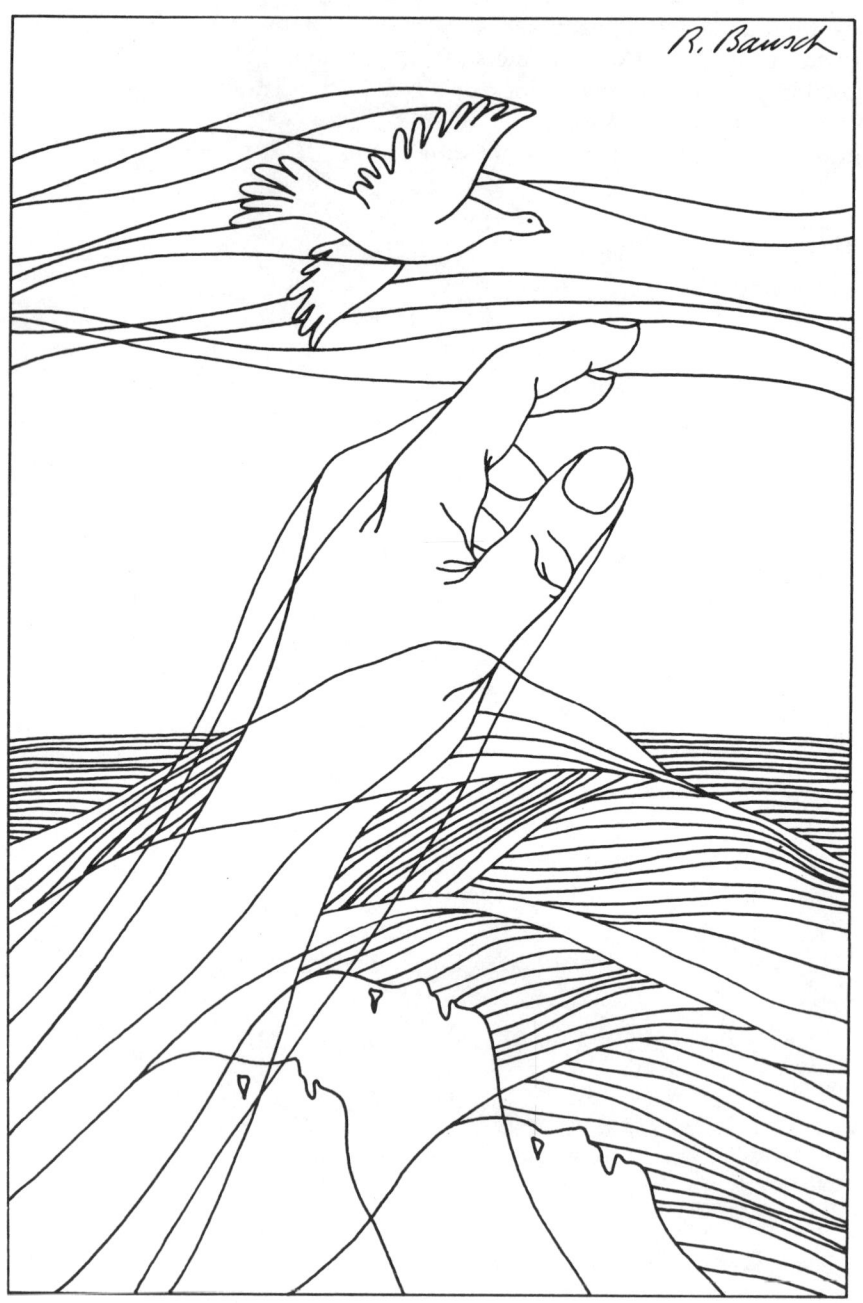

BLOWIN' IN THE WIND

How many roads must a man walk down
Before you call him a man?
Yes and how many seas must a white dove sail
Before she sleeps in the sand?
Yes and how many times must the cannon balls fly
Before they're forever banned?
    The answer, my friend, is blowin' in the wind,
    The answer is blowin' in the wind.

How many times must a man look up
Before he can see the sky?
Yes and how many ears must one man have
Before he can hear people cry?
Yes and how many deaths will it take till he knows
That too many people have died?
    The answer, my friend, is blowin' in the wind,
    The answer is blowin' in the wind.

How many years can a mountain exist
Before it's washed to the sea?
Yes and how many years can some people exist
Before they're allowed to be free?
Yes and how many times can a man turn his head
Pretending he just doesn't see?
    The answer, my friend, is blowin' in the wind,
    The answer is blowin' in the wind.

—Bob Dylan

BOB DYLAN

Writing about Bob Dylan is writing about being young. It is not writing about youth, or the youth culture, or anything so abstract, but about *being* young, about the intense years between eleven and twenty. Not all popular music is young music. Many country-and-western songs talk about disappointments and resignations that belong psychologically if not chronologically to the middle years. The blues often express a misery so pure that the singer seems old and so wise in the unjust ways of the world that he is beyond both disappointment and resignation. But the sixties music of Dylan and the Beatles and the Rolling Stones is young music, full of energy, combativeness, anger, and delight, such as in "Michele," "I'm Looking Through You," "Something Happened to Me Yesterday," "Sympathy for the Devil," "Like a Rolling Stone" and "The Times They Are A-Changin"; when you hear Dylan or the Beatles or the Stones you feel your own young passions.

The sort of intense feeling that popular songs can bring back—an emotion sexual, reverent, vast, fierce, tender, and more—is what much of poetry is "about." Ezra Pound once said that literature is language charged with meaning. Meaning is not a kind of addition to language, not a toting up of symbols and equivalents (as if in a school yell: "Give me a C, give me an A, give me a C-A-T, give me a FOUR-LEGGED, SMALL AND FURRY ANIMAL THAT PURRS"). Meaning is feeling, too, and intense feeling at that. And it is everywhere, like an electric current in the language. Dylan's songs can seem so meaningful they burn. How can one explain it?

In a sense the mystery is not in Dylan, or even in his songs, but in his audience. They give him their intensity, their emotion. Dylan himself speaks very matter-of-factly about what he does as a poet, songwriter, performer, and musician. His attitude may seem so matter of fact that one wonders, "Can he be real? Can he be as plain and simple as all that? Is he putting us on?" but these questions tell more about the expectations and fears of the audience than they do about Dylan. To illustrate, when Jann Wenner, Editor of *Rolling Stone,* asks Dylan about tours and performances, he has in mind Dylan's powerful attractiveness to an immense audience.* But when Dylan talks about tours and performances, what *he* thinks about is how hard it is to remember all the words in all the verses, or how difficult it is to keep up his own intensity of feeling and presence throughout a performance or which songs the audiences like. Mike Bloomfield, a musician who has worked with Dylan, has said that when he is recording Dylan fixes on clarity: Are the words delivered clearly? Will the audience be able to hear them well? Another example: Many people feel that for the *Nashville Skyline* album Dylan changed his style to a remarkable degree. When Wenner asked why he changed, Dylan explained that he had quit smoking and that he was surprised as anything to find out what a difference it made in his voice.

Dylan leaves interpretive work to his audience. The audience must decide whether to like the song and how to like it and what it means. Orpheus in

Rolling Stone, November 29, 1969. See especially pp. 23, 27, and 31.

the Greek myth is as simple as Dylan. Orpheus played the lute; he liked to play the lute. When his wife Eurydice died, he missed her very much, so he offered the gods of the underworld an exchange: He would play for them if they would give him Eurydice. Why did they accept? Why did the stones weep when he played, and why did the gods so want to hear him that he alone of the living was permitted to walk in and out of Hell? Dylan himself seems not to understand why his audiences treat him as they do.

In interviews Dylan disclaims any special gifts of wisdom or moral strength. He is modest, decent, and a family man. He doesn't take up with the power of Satanism, like Mick Jagger, or with the power of politics, like John Lennon. Yet he moves in a field of intense emotion. If audiences care about what Dylan does, says, and means, and if Dylan stands for the feeling of being young in each of us, these things come about, at least in part, as a consequence of Dylan's integrity. We believe that he does not make compromises with his sense of himself, that he is as pure as a twelve-year-old, as pure as Huckleberry Finn. We believe that there is good reason to feel that Dylan possesses youthful virtues of being able to respect himself and to maintain his identity.

In the fall of 1968 a young Dylan freak named Toby Thompson left school and set off for Dylan's home town of Hibbing, a small town in northeastern Minnesota, some hundred miles from the Canadian border. (Dylan was born in Duluth in 1951.) He met teachers and friends who remembered Dylan, visited the family home (recently sold), met a charming girlfriend named Echo, and spoke with Dylan's brother David. He published an account of the trip in *The Village Voice* newspaper in 1969. Later he returned to Minnesota, again to Hibbing, but also to Minneapolis, where Dylan had spent several months at the University of Minnesota. There Thompson met a girl who had been Dylan's friend in college. In Hibbing he had lunch with Dylan's mother. The story of these journeys is told in the book *Positively Main Street* (Coward-McCann, Inc., 1971).

Several circumstances stand out in Thompson's account of his adventure: the decency and kindness with which he was received by the people he met, the affection within Dylan's family, and the consistency and integrity of Bob Dylan himself. Although Thompson puts to rest some "facts" about Dylan (for instance, that he ran away from home many times), the Dylan he finds in Hibbing is of a piece with the Dylan who now lives near Woodstock. He describes a Dylan whose ambition, as recorded in his high school yearbook, was to join Little Richard, a Dylan who listened late at night to rock and roll music—to Chuck Berry, Fats Domino, Little Richard, and Jimmy Reed—from a black radio station in Little Rock, Arkansas. In 1957, his eleventh grade year, Dylan had a band. Dylan and the band performed, very loud, in the Hibbing High Jacket Jambourie Talent Festival. Dylan shouted and sang and played (piano) standing up. He broke a foot pedal off the piano. Some people booed and some laughed, the music was so strange. In 1960 at the University of Minnesota Dylan, who had grown up as Bob (or Robert or Bobby) Zimmerman, son of the owner of a furniture and appliance store, had no band, but he did play guitar at parties, and he called himself Dylan. He seemed more a follower of Woody Guthrie than of Little Richard. A girl who knew him during his months in Minneapolis recalls that he was teased for his devotion to Guthrie's art. In those days people drank wine and beer at parties. Late in an evening someone might say to Bob, "Woody's outside, he wants to meet you," and Bob might go out looking for Woody. (He did visit Guthrie in a New Jersey hospital before the composer died in 1967 after a long illness.) In the winter of 1960-1961 Dylan asked to leave the University and Hibbing for New York City. His parents gave him the little help he needed. In New York he got what work he could singing in small folk music clubs. Robert Shelton, a reporter for *The New York Times*, heard him perform and praised him vigorously in a review.* Dylan's success in clubs soon led to his recording for Columbia records. His first album, *Bob Dylan* (1962), was a performance album, but his second, *The Freewheelin' Bob Dylan* (1963), was all Dylan songs. "Blowin' in the Wind," a song on that album, became Dylan's first great hit.

Dylan's integrity is closely related to another quality, tact, a form of respect for the individuality of others. In a world of images and publicity, talk shows and propaganda, Dylan is a man who keeps his opinions to himself. He does not seek interviews, nor, when he gives one, does he tell others what they ought to think or feel, even about Dylan. One might begin to feel that he is withdrawn and elusive, but if one reads Nat Hentoff's interview in *Playboy* (March 1966), one might also feel that Dylan is only trying to keep a sense of balance, a sense of values. The questions Hentoff poses invite Dylan to explain all kinds of things, but Dylan always seems to remember that he is a song writer, not a teacher, preacher, prophet, or sociologist. Hentoff asks Dylan why it is the age group from 16 to 25 that listens to his songs. Dylan replies that he didn't think it would be the age group between 85 and 90. Hentoff asks whether Dylan would like to help all those young people, to keep them from turning into what their parents have become. Dylan says he doesn't know their parents, and he doesn't know if anybody's parents are so bad. Hentoff asks how Dylan feels when people call his clothing oddball and sloppy and defiant. Dylan answers that there's a war on, that people have rickets and cancer.

In the film *Don't Look Back* D. A. Pennebaker records Dylan's concert tour of England in April and May of 1965. At the London Airport a reporter greets Dylan with "What is your real message?"* Another asks, "Do you ever read the Bible?" A reporter for *Time* wonders, "Do you care about what you sing?" Even Jann Wenner asks questions that could encourage Dylan to pose as a hero and a youth leader. What does Dylan think about all the people who feel deeply affected by his music? Does he feel responsible toward them? Dylan answers that he is not a leader of youth, that if he thought he were a leader, he'd be out there leading. The Maharishi, he says, thinks he's a leader of youth, and that's what he does, he leads. Dylan isn't *trained* to be a youth leader. "I play music, man. I write songs. I have a certain balance about things."†

*With Dylan's cooperation Shelton and his wife are writing a biography of Dylan.

*This and the following quotations are from a transcript of the D. A. Pennebaker film, *Don't Look Back* (New York: Ballantine Books, 1968), pp. 21, 25, and 128.
†*Rolling Stone* (November 29, 1969), p. 27.

Dylan's creative energy, like all creative energy, has its limits as to what it can achieve; Dylan is indeed a poet and song writer, but he has written a sort of novel, *Tarantula* (Macmillan, 1971), and he has, in a manner of speaking, engaged in literary criticism. His career as a critic was brief. His statement that Smokey Robinson (of Smokey Robinson and the Miracles) was the greatest modern poet has been widely reported; but in his interview with Jann Wenner he explained, "I didn't mean Smokey Robinson. I meant Arthur Rimbaud. I don't know how I could've gotten Smokey Robinson mixed up with Arthur Rimbaud."*

Tarantula comes from one of the social forms of Dylan's integrity, his love of the put-on, that deadpan dishonesty that can test the integrity (and the intelligence) of others (and can also be simply zany and playful). Reporters used to ask him, he says, whether he wrote anything else. And he'd answer no. And they would say, oh come on, you must write other things, do you write books? And he'd say, oh, sure, books. When publishers learned that he wrote books, they would send him contracts: first they would pay him, then he would write the book. Dylan signed a contract and put together a book during a week on the road, adding to it whatever the folks around the hotel room had to put in it. When he delivered the manuscript to the publishers, they did not say thank you for the book, it's terrible, we won't print it, and please don't write another. Instead, they told him what a fine book he had written. This response angered Dylan: "It wasn't about anything . . . and I knew that—I figured they *had* to know that, they were in the business of it. I knew that, and I was just nobody. If I knew it, where were they at? They were just playing with me."* The book itself embarrassed him; so instead of correcting the proofs when he received them, he wrote another book. The publisher said all right. But when he saw the proofs of the new book, he didn't like it, either, so he started to revise again. It was at this time that he had his motorcycle accident and broke several vertebrae in his neck. The accident changed him somehow, in mind as well as in body, and he was not able to pick up his life where he had left it. The book was still incomplete, but he decided not to finish it. The publishers could have sued him to recover the money they had given him before he wrote anything for them, but they chose instead to publish the first manuscript, *Tarantula*.

The songs included here come from *The Freewheelin' Bob Dylan* (1963), *Another Side of Bob Dylan* (1964), *Bringing It All Back Home* (1965), *Nashville Skyline* (1969), and *New Morning* (1970).

*Rolling Stone.
*Rolling Stone.

IT AIN'T ME, BABE

Go away from my window,
Leave at your own chosen speed.
I'm not the one you want, babe,
I'm not the one you need.
You say you're looking for someone
Who's never weak but always strong
To protect you and defend you
Whether you are right or wrong,
Someone to open each and every door,
    But it ain't me, babe,
    No no no it ain't me, babe,
    It ain't me you're looking for, babe.

Go lightly from the ledge, babe,
Go lightly on the ground,
I'm not the one you want, babe,
I will only let you down.
You say you're looking for someone
Who will promise never to part,
Someone to close his eyes for you,
Someone to close his heart,
Someone who will die for you and more,
    But it ain't me, babe,
    No no no it ain't me, babe,
    It ain't me you're looking for, babe.

Go melt back into the night,
Everything inside is made of stone,
There's nothing in here moving
An' anyway I'm not alone.
You say you're looking for someone
Who'll pick you up each time you fall,
To gather flowers constantly
And to come each time you call,
A lover for your life and nothing more,
    But it ain't me, babe,
    No no no it ain't me, babe,
    It ain't me you're looking for, babe.

1964

SUBTERRANEAN HOMESICK BLUES

Johnny's in the basement
Mixing up the medicine
I'm on the pavement
Thinking about the government
The man in the trenchcoat
Badge out, laid off
Says he's got a bad cough
Wants to get it paid off
Look out kid
It's something you did
God knows when
But you're doin' it again
You better duck down the alleyway
Lookin' for a new friend
The man in the coonskin cap
By the big pen
Wants eleven dollar bills
You only got ten.

Maggie comes fleet foot
Face full of black soot
Talkin' at the heat put
Plants in the bed but
The phone's tapped anyway
Maggie says that many say
They must bust in early May
Orders from the D.A.
Look out kid
Don't matter what you did
Walk on your tip toes
Don't try "No Doz"
Better stay away from those
That carry around a fire hose
Keep a clean nose
Watch the plain clothes
You don't need a weather man
To know which way the wind blows.

Get sick get well
Hang around an ink well

Ring bell, hard to tell
If anything is goin' to sell
Try hard, get barred
Get back, write braille
Get jailed, jump bail
Join the army, if you fail
Look out kid, you're gonna get hit
But users, cheaters
Six time losers
Hang around the theatres
Girl by the whirlpool
Lookin' for a new fool
Don't follow leaders
Watch the parkin' meters.

Ah, get born, keep warm
Short pants, romance, learn to dance
Get dressed, get blessed
Try to be a success
Please her, please him, buy gifts
Don't steal, don't lift
Twenty years of schoolin'
And they put you on the day shift
Look out kid, they keep it all hid
Better jump down a manhole
Light yourself a candle, don't wear sandals
Try to avoid the scandals
Don't wanna be a bum
You better chew gum
The pump don't work
'Cause the vandals took the handles.

1965

MR. TAMBOURINE MAN

Hey Mr. Tambourine Man, play a song for me
I'm not sleepy and there is no place I'm goin' to,
Hey Mr. Tambourine Man, play a song for me
In the jingle jangle mornin' I'll come followin' you.

Though I know that evenin's empire has returned into sand,
Vanished from my hand,
Left me blindly here to stand but still not sleepin'.
My weariness amazes me, I am branded on my feet,
I have no one to meet
And the ancient empty street's too dead for dreamin'.

Hey Mr. Tambourine Man, play a song for me
I'm not sleepy and there is no place I'm goin' to,
Hey Mr. Tambourine Man, play a song for me
In the jingle jangle mornin' I'll come followin' you.

Take me on a trip upon your magic swirlin' ship,
My senses have been stripped, my hands can't feel to grip,
My toes too numb to step, wait only for my boot heels
To be wanderin'.
I'm ready to go anywhere, I'm ready for to fade
Into my own parade, cast your dancin' spell my way
I promise to go under it.

Hey Mr. Tambourine Man, play a song for me
I'm not sleepy and there is no place I'm goin' to,
Hey Mr. Tambourine Man, play a song for me
In the jingle jangle mornin' I'll come followin' you.

Though you might hear laughin' spinnin' swingin' madly across the sun,
It's not aimed at anyone, it's just escapin' on the run
And but for the sky there are no fences facin',
And if you hear vague traces of skippin' reels of rhyme
To your tambourine in time, it's just a ragged clown behind
I wouldn't pay it any mind, it's just a shadow you're
Seein' that he's chasin'.

Hey Mr. Tambourine Man, play a song for me
I'm not sleepy and there is no place I'm goin' to,
Hey Mr. Tambourine Man, play a song for me
In the jingle jangle mornin' I'll come followin' you.

Then take me disappearin' through the smoke rings of my mind
Down the foggy ruins of time, far past the frozen leaves,
The haunted, frightened trees, out to the windy beach
Far from the twisted reach of crazy sorrow,
Yes to dance beneath the diamond sky with one hand wavin' free

BOB DYLAN

Silhouetted by the sea, circled by the circus sands
With all memory and fate driven deep beneath the waves
Let me forget about today until tomorrow.

Hey Mr. Tambourine Man, play a song for me
I'm not sleepy and there is no place I'm goin' to,
Hey Mr. Tambourine Man, play a song for me
In the jingle jangle mornin' I'll come followin' you.

1965

LAY, LADY, LAY

Lay, lady, lay, lay across my big brass bed
Lay, lady, lay, lay across my big brass bed
Whatever colors you have in your mind
I'll show them to you and you'll see them shine

Lay, lady, lay, lay across my big brass bed
Stay, lady, stay, stay with your man awhile
Until the break of day, let me see you make him smile
His clothes are dirty but his hands are clean
And you're the best thing that he's ever seen

Stay, lady, stay, stay with your man awhile
Why wait any longer for the world to begin
You can have your cake and eat it too
Why wait any longer for the one you love
When he's standing in front of you

Lay, lady, lay, lay across my big brass bed
Stay, lady, stay, stay while the night is still ahead
I long to see you in the morning light
I long to reach for you in the night
Stay, lady, stay, stay while the night is still ahead

1969

IF DOGS RUN FREE

If dogs run free, then why not we
Across the swooping plain?
My ears hear a symphony
Of two mules, trains and rain.
The best is always yet to come,
That's what they explain to me.
Just do your thing, you'll be king,
If dogs run free.

If dogs run free, why not me
Across the swamp of time?
My mind weaves a symphony
And tapestry of rhyme.
Oh, winds which rush my tale to thee
So it may flow and be.
To each his own, it's all unknown
If dogs run free.

If dogs run free, then what must be,
Must be, and that is all.
True love can make a blade of grass
Stand up straight and tall.
In harmony with the cosmic sea,
True love needs no company;
It can cure the soul, it can make it whole
If dogs run free.

1970

PAUL SIMON

Paul Simon (1941, Queens, New York) wrote a hit song, "Hey Schoolgirl," in 1957 with his friend Art Garfunkel. He and Garfunkel were then performing together under the names Tom and Jerry. After the success of Bob Dylan, the two made an album in the folk style, *Wednesday Morning 3 A.M.* (1964). On the album were some songs by Dylan and some by Simon. One of them—"The Sound of Silence"—caught the attention of a disc jockey and then of a producer at Columbia records who saw to it that the song was made into a single record, and it became a hit.

THE SOUND OF SILENCE*

Hello darkness my old friend,
I've come to talk with you again,
Because a vision softly creeping,
Left its seeds while I was sleeping
And the vision that was planted in my brain
Still remains within the sound of silence.

In restless dreams I walked alone,
Narrow streets of cobble stone
'Neath the halo of a street lamp,
I turned my collar to the cold and damp
When my eyes were stabbed by the flash of a neon light
That split the night, and touched the sound of silence.

And in the naked light I saw
Ten thousand people maybe more,
People talking without speaking,
People hearing without listening,
People writing songs that voices never share
And no one dares disturb the sound of silence.

* © copyright 1964 by Paul Simon. Used with the permission of the Publisher.

"Fools!" said I, "You do not know
Silence like a cancer grows.
Hear my words that I might teach you
Take my arms that I might reach you."
But my words like silent raindrops fell
And echoed, in the wells of silence.

And the people bowed and prayed
To the neon God they made,
And the sign flashed out its warning
In the words that it was forming.
And the sign said:
      "The words of the prophets are written
        on the subway walls and tenement halls"
And whispered in the sound of silence.

1964

DON L. LEE

Don L. Lee (1942, Little Rock, Arkansas) founded the Third World Press and publishes *Black Expression,* a literary journal. He is a staff member of the Museum of African-American History in Chicago and a teacher of Afro-American literature at Columbia (he attended Roosevelt University, Chicago). In 1969 he was writer in residence at Cornell. The poems are from *Think Black* (1967) and *Don't Cry, Scream* (1969).

IN A PERIOD OF GROWTH

like,
if he had da called me
black seven years ago,
i wd've—
        broke his right eye out,
        jumped into his chest,
        talked about his momma,
        lied on his sister
        & dared him to say it again

all in one breath—

seven years ago.

ASSASSINATION

    it was wild.
    the
    bullet hit high.
                (the throat-neck)

  & from everywhere:
    the motel, from under bushes and cars,
    from around corners and across streets,
    out of the garbage cans and from rat holes
    in the earth

they came running.
with
guns
drawn
they came running
toward the King—
    all of them
    fast and sure—

as if
the King
was going to fire back.
they came running,
fast and sure,
in the
wrong
direction.

THE REVOLUTIONARY SCREW
(FOR MY BLACKSISTERS)

brothers,
i
under/overstand
the situation:

i mean—
  u bes hitten the man hard
  all day long.
a stone revolutionary, "a full time revolutionary."
  tellen the man how bad u is
  & what u goin ta do
  & how u goin ta do it.

it must be a bitch
to be able to do all that
talken. (& not one irregular breath fr/yr mouth)
being so
forceful & all
to the man's face (the courage)
& u not even cracken a smile (realman).

i know,
the sisters just don't
understand the
pressure u is under.

&
when u ask for a piece
of leg/
it's not for yr/self
but for
yr/people——it keeps u going
& anyway u is a revolutionary

& she wd be doin
a revolutionary thing.

that sister dug it
from the beginning,
had an early-eye.
i mean
she really had it together
when she said:
     go fuck yr/self nigger.

now
that was
revolutionary.

JOHN BALABAN

John Balaban was born in 1943 in Philadelphia. He went to school at Penn State and Harvard, and he now teaches at Penn State. He served two years in Vietnam as a conscientious objector, first as an instructor at the University of Can Tho in the Mekong Delta, and later as a field representative for the Committee of Responsibility to Save War-Injured Children. In 1971 he returned to Vietnam as a representative of the Committee. "The Guard at the Binh Thuy Bridge" comes from *Vietnam Poems* (1970).

THE GUARD AT THE BINH THUY BRIDGE

How still he stands as mists begin to move,
as morning, curling, billows creep across
his coop-like, concrete sentry perched mid-bridge
over mid-muddy-river. Stares at bush-green banks
which bristle rifles, mortars, men—perhaps.
No convoys shake the timbers. No sound
but water slapping boatsides, banksides, pilings.
He's slung his carbine barrel down to keep
the boring dry, and two banana-clips instead of one
are taped to make, now, forty rounds instead
of twenty. Droplets bead from stock to sight;
they bulb, then strike his boot. He scrapes his heel,
and sees no boxbombs floating towards his bridge.
Anchored in red morning mist a narrow junk
rocks its weight. A woman kneels on deck
staring at lapping water. Wets her face.
Idly the thick Rach Binh Thuy slides by.
He aims. At her. Then drops his aim. Idly.

JIM MORRISON

Jim Morrison was lead singer with The Doors. He was born in 1946 in Los Angeles (?), and he died in 1971 in Paris. He attended the University of California, Los Angeles. He wrote a screen play with Michael McClure, a poet living in San Francisco, "The Adept," which is yet to be performed. He is also the author of a book of poems, *Feast of Friends*. He began writing poetry when he was very young, but became a song writer during the height of the popularity of rock music. "The End" was recorded in January 1967. It appears on the album *The Doors* (Elektra EKL-4007).

THE END*

This is the end,
Beautiful friend,
This is the end,
My only friend,
The end of our elaborate plans,
The end of everything that stands,
The end. No safety or surprise,
The end. I'll never look into your eyes
Again.

Can you picture what will be,
So limitless and free,
Desperately in need of some stranger's hand
In a desperate land.
Lost in a Roman wilderness of pain
And all the children are insane
All the children are insane;
Waiting for the summer rain.

There's danger on the edge of town,
Ride the king's highway.

* ℗ copyright 1967 Doors Music Co. Used by permission of the Author and Publisher. All rights reserved.

Weird scenes inside the gold mine;
Ride the king's highway west, baby.
Ride the snake
To the lake
The ancient lake.
The snake is long
Seven miles;
Ride the snake,
He's old and his skin is cold.

The West is the best
The West is the best.
Get here and we'll do the rest.
The blue bus is calling us.
Driver, where you taking us?

The killer awoke before dawn,
He put his boots on,
He took a face from the ancient gallery,
And he walked on down the hall.
He went to the room where his sister lived,
And then he paid a visit to his brother,
And then he walked on down the hall.
And he came to a door.
And he looked inside

"Father?"
"Yes, son?"
"I want to kill you."
"Mother, I want to . . ."

Come on baby, take a chance with us,
And meet me by the back of the blue bus.

This is the end,
Beautiful friend.
This is the end,
My only friend, the end.
It hurts to set you free
But you'll never follow me
The end of laughter and soft lies,
The end of night we tried to die.
This is the end.

VICTOR HERNÁNDEZ CRUZ

Victor Cruz was born in 1949 in Aguas Buenas, Puerto Rico, but has lived in New York City since 1954. He attended Benjamin Franklin High School in East Harlem where he led a Free Speech Movement. He has been an editor of *Umbra* magazine and a playwright with the Gut-Theatre in East Harlem. The poems are from *Snaps* (1969).

& STUFF LIKE THAT

it was
a year ago
tricks were
played all over
i got it
two times
ten dollars
i lost
bombs all over
the same cat
won't pull it twice
on the same sucker
unless he was
a pad boy
then they may
pull it on him
a million times
before he got hip
nothing you could do
unless you sight the guy
& cut him

but
the best thing
is to be tight
with the main man
this way
      you get good stuff
      & you'll do the tricks.

IS A DEAD MAN

hopeless
useless
the sound makes
me tremble run
for cover   run
till I hear it
no longer   till
the thought of
it spilling is
gone it will
turn me to soft
yellow to talk
like a bird
all these grown
men i must stare
at all these
guilty bodies
waving at me
coming out the
t.v. set   why
they sing in
silence   they
cook in caves
they kiss with
plastic covers
they dance like
shit is coming
out they ass
or like they
all retarded
why don't i
just cut one &
see if they for
real   they for
real lord they
for real you
gots to live with
this   you gots to
talk with this you
gots to play with
this   in your mind

VICTOR HERNÁNDEZ CRUZ

drop it out you
mind shit
stomp the shit
to the air out
your precious head
out your life
it is there
they live
they have books
they have bands
god help us they
have bands   they
have singers   O
they have singers
who knock you into
orbit   around boredom
snag at the moon
forget they exist
forget they talk
forget where you are
if they come to
your door to sing
& play noise   then
you bang them people
up   blow them up
snap their necks
eat their brains out
burn their eyes out
knuckles away
knuckles away
send them fags fly-
ing thru air

hopeless
useless
is a dead
dead world
they selling
here.

LATIN & SOUL

for Joe Bataan
1

some waves
          a wave of now
                    a trombone speaking to you
a piano is trying to break a molecule
is trying to lift the stage into orbit
around the red spotlights

a shadow
the shadows   of dancers
dancers   they are dancing   falling
out that space   made for dancing

they should dance
on the tables   they should
dance inside of their drinks
they should dance on the
ceiling they should dance/dance

thru universes
leaning-moving
                  we are traveling

where are we going
if we only knew

with this rhythm   with
this banging   with   fire
with this   all   this   O
my god i wonder   where are

we going
          sink into a room full of laughter
          full of happiness   full of life
          those dancers
          the dancers

VICTOR HERNÁNDEZ CRUZ

                        are clapping their hands
                        stomping their feet
hold back them tears
                all those sentimental stories
    cooked uptown   if you can   hold it for after

we are going
            away-away-away
            beyond these wooden tables
            beyond these red lights
            beyond these rugs & paper
            walls   beyond   way past
            i mean way past them clouds
            over the buildings   over the
            rivers   over towns   over cities
            like on rails   but faster   like
            a train   but smoother
            away past stars
            bursting with drums.

2

a sudden misunderstanding
                        a cloud
                        full of grayness
a body thru a store window
                    a hand reaching
                    into the back

                                            pocket
        a scream
                    a piano is talking to you
                    thru all this
                    why don't you answer it.

LIST OF RECORDINGS BY POETS

For song recordings, consult the *Schwann Record & Tape Guide* (formerly *Schwann Record Catalogue*).

Many of the poets included here have made recordings of their poems at the Library of Congress in Washington, D.C. Some of these recordings from the Library's archive are available on discs, some on magnetic tape. Some records and tapes are for sale, some are not, depending upon the agreement reached between the recording poet and the Library. For information as to the availability and cost of the Library of Congress recordings listed below, write to

> Chief, General Reference and Bibliography Division
> Library of Congress
> Washington, D.C. 20540.

For tapes available from radio station KPFA in Berkeley, California, write to

> Director, Pacifica Tape Library
> 2217 Shattuck Avenue
> Berkeley, Ca. 94704.

For tapes available from radio station WBAI in New York City write to

> WBAI
> 359 East 62nd St.
> New York, N.Y. 10021.

For tapes available from McGraw-Hill Book Company, write to

> Mr. David Berquist
> McGraw-Hill Book Company
> 330 West 42nd St.
> New York, N.Y. 10036.

For the sake of economy, the entries have been abbreviated. Library of Congress is abbreviated LC. LC entries contain a catalogue number ("cat.") and a Library Work Order number ("LWO"). They include also a date and, if the recording were made elsewhere than at the Library, a place of recording. The Library has made some long-playing records. These are listed as "LC record."

Commercial recordings are listed, where possible, by record number only.

Imamu Amiri Baraka (LeRoi Jones). LC cat. 391, LWO 2831 (Apr. 17, 1959).
  A tape recording of a reading given (together with Gwendolyn Brooks) at the Asilomar (Calif.) Negro Writers Conference (summer 1964) is available from KPFA.

Robert Bly. LC cat. 87, LWO 3106 (May 2, 1960).

Gwendolyn Brooks. LC cat. 109, LWO 3237 (Jan. 19, 1961). Also LC cat. 110, LWO 2863, reel 2 (YMHA Poetry Center, NYC, with Peter Viereck; includes "Beverly Hills, Chicago"). A tape recording of a reading given (together with LeRoi Jones) at the Asilomar (Calif.) Negro Writers Conference (summer 1964) is available from KPFA.

Gregory Corso. LC cat. 164, LWO 2799 (Feb. 27, 1969).

Robert Creeley. LC cat. 168, LWO 3348 (June 1, 1961; includes "If You" and "I Know a Man"). A tape recording of a reading given at the YMHA Poetry Center, NYC, is available from McGraw-Hill (reel-to-reel: 78153; cassette: 81664).

E. E. Cummings. LC record: P L5 (1953). Also on Caedmon records TC 2006 and Columbia records ML 4259.

James Dickey. Spoken Arts records 984.

Robert Duncan. LC cat. 207, LWO 2058 (Berkeley, Ca., Mar. 22, 1952).

Lawrence Ferlinghetti. Fantasy LP 7004 (includes "In Goya's Greatest Scenes"). "After the Cries of the Birds" is available on tape from KPFA. Also Fantasy LP *Jazz and Poetry at the Cellar* (with Kenneth Rexroth; San Francisco, 1959).

Allen Ginsberg. Fantasy LP 7006 (includes "A Supermarket in California," "America," and "Sunflower Sutra"). Also Gramophone (England) PSY30002 (May 1968; includes "Wales—Visitation 29th July 1967").

Randall Jarrell. LC cat. 378, LWO 2689, reel 6 (June 9, 1947; includes "The Death of the Ball Turret Gunner"). Also LC record: P L7 (1954). Also on LC record P24. A tape recording of a reading given at the San Francisco State College Poetry Center is available from KPFA.

Weldon Kees. LC cat. 396, LWO 2058 (Berkeley, Ca., Mar. 22, 1952).

Kenneth Koch. LC cat. 406, LWO 3111 (May 9, 1960).

Denise Levertov. LC cat. 429, LWO 2882 (June 15, 1958). Also in the collection of the Poetry Room, Lamont Library, Harvard University (LP and tape). Also WBAI tape. Also KPFA tape (University of California at Berkeley, Nov. 10, 1961).

Robert Lowell. LC record PL 22. Also on Yale Series of Recorded Poets, Carillon records YP 301. Also KPFA tape (San Francisco Museum of Art, May 1966).

W. S. Merwin. LC cat. 497, LWO 2932 (Fassett Recording Studios, Boston, Mass., Mar. 18, 1958). Also LC cat. 498, LWO 3309 (Coolidge Auditorium, Apr. 10, 1961).

Josephine Miles. LC cat. 503, LWO 2930 (Berkeley, Ca., Sept. 20, 1958; includes "Autumnal").

Marianne Moore. LC records PL 2 and PL 20. Also KPFA tape (University of California at Berkeley).

Sylvia Plath. LC cat. 576, LWO 2939 (Springfield, Mass., Apr. 18, 1958). Also Gramophone (England) PLP 1085.

Ezra Pound. Caedmon records TC 1122 and 1155. The latter includes "Canto XLV."

Theodore Roethke. LC records PL 10 (1954; includes last two sections of "The Lost Son"), PL 22 and PL 29. Also Folkways LP record FL 9736.

Anne Sexton. McGraw-Hill tape (YMHA, NYC).

Gary Snyder. KPFA tape (University of California at Berkeley).

William Stafford. LC cat. 714, LWO 2928 (Lewis and Clark College, Portland, Oregon, Sept. 18, 1958).

Diane Wakoski. LC cat. 793, LWO 3993, reel 5, side B (NYC, radio station WEVD, Feb. 5, 1961).

Jonathan Williams. LC cat. 828, LWO 4630 (June 18, 1965). Also Folkways Records: "Blues & Roots/Rue & Bluets (Jonathan Williams Reads His Poems." (summer 1964).

William Carlos Williams. LC records P L4 and PL 20. Also Caedmon records TC 1047. Also Columbia records ML 4259. Also KPFA tape (University of California at Berkeley, May 1955).

James Wright. LC cat. 845, LWO 2891 (May 25, 1958).

AUTHOR INDEX

Balaban, John 249
Baraka, Imamu Amiri 200
Berry, Chuck 204
Bly, Robert 132
Brooks, Gwendolyn 56

Clifton, Lucille 211
Cooke, Sam 198
Corso, Gregory 157
Cruz, Victor Hernández 252
Creeley, Robert 125
Cropper, Steve. *See* Redding, Otis. 230
Cummings, E. E. 23

Dickey, James 81
Duncan, Robert 75
Dylan, Bob 234

Elon, Florence 224

Ferlinghetti, Lawrence 66
Field, Edward 89

Ginsberg, Allen 110
Guthrie, Woody 40

Hayden, Robert 44

Jarrell, Randall 54
Johnson, J.C. *See* Smith, Bessie. 21
Jones, LeRoi. *See* Baraka, Imamu Amiri. 200

Kaufman, Bob 102
Kees, Weldon 50
Koch, Kenneth 96

Lee, Don L. 246
Levertov, Denise 85

Lowell, Robert 60

Merwin, W. S. 144
Miles, Josephine 36
Moore, Marianne 19
Morrison, Jim 250

Neruda, Pablo. *See* Bly, Robert. 132

O'Hara, Frank 123
Olson, Charles 31

Plath, Sylvia 178
Pound, Ezra 13

Redding, Otis 230
Reed, Ishmael 218
Rich, Adrienne 154
Roethke, Theodore 25

Sanchez, Sonia 209
Sanders, Zel 208
Schuyler, James 87
Seeger, Pete 73
Sexton, Anne 146
Slick, Grace 228
Smith, Bessie 21
Simic, Charles 221
Simon, Paul 244
Snyder, Gary 162
Spector, Lona. *See* Stevens, Lona. 208
Stafford, William 53
Stevens, Lona 208

Wakoski, Diane 214
Welch, James 226
Williams, Jonathan 153
Williams, William Carlos 8
Wright, James 141